O THE TIMES!
O THE MANNERS!

by the same author

THE PIOUS PORNOGRAPHERS

O THE TIMES!
O THE MANNERS!

by WILLIAM IVERSEN

William Morrow & Co. New York, 1965

All six chapters of this book have appeared in different form, as separate articles in *Playboy*.

Published simultaneously in the Dominion of Canada by George J. McLeod Limited, Toronto.

Printed in the United States of America.

Library of Congress Catalog Card Number 64-23583

Contents

The author wishes to express his gratitude and indebtedness to the two hundred and more authors whose books, articles, essays, plays, poems and news reports have contributed to the writing of this book. Wherever possible, sources have been acknowledged within the body of the text.

PREFACE

Preface

"History, after all, is valuable only in so far as it lives . . ." Eileen Power declared in the preface to her now-classic *Medieval People.* "It is the idea that history is about dead people, or, worse still, about movements and conditions which seem but vaguely related to the labors and passions of flesh and blood, which has driven history from bookshelves where the historical novel still finds a welcome place."

Something of the same thought had been expressed more than two decades before in the salty Irish-American idiom of Finley Peter Dunne's legendary bartender, Mr. Dooley: "I know histhry isn't thrue, Hinnessy, because it ain't like what I see ivry day in Halsted Sthreet. If any wan comes along with a histhry iv Greece or Rome that'll show me th' people fightin', gettin' dhrunk, makin' love, gettin' married, owin' the grocery man an' bein' without hard-coal, I'll believe they was a Greece or Rome, but not befure. Historyans is like doctors. They are always lookin' f'r symptoms. Those iv them that writes about their own times examines th' tongue an' feels th' pulse an' makes a wrong dygnosis. Th' other kind iv histhry is a post-mortem examination. It tells ye what a counthry died iv. But I'd like to know what it lived iv."

For better or worse, this small book of histories is of the Dooley school, and is the product of one man's curiosity concerning some of the ordinary, everyday things that people have "lived iv." It was written out of a personal belief that the study of wars, governments and world-shaking events often reveals far less of historical Man than does a knowledge of the money he used, the oaths he swore, the jigs he danced, the toasts he drank, the ways he wore his hair, and his attitudes toward bathing. These are among the more enduring things—the persistent trifles and preoccupations that we share with men of all Ages.

I

MONEY

Money

Money is undoubtedly the most popular of all ancient conveniences. Whether we consider it to be the root of all evil or the source of all that is jolly and good, there's no denying the advantages that money has over earlier systems of swap and barter. Anyone who has ever attempted to pay a fifty-cent taxi fare with a ten-dollar bill can readily imagine the difficulties that might arise in trying to get a cabdriver to make change of an ox—to say nothing of having to compute a tip in terms of broccoli and rhubarb.

Applied to modern urban living, such a system would prove both unwieldy and absurd. But no more absurd, perhaps, than some of the peculiar forms of money that men have been known to hoard and fret about: shells, feathers, beads, stones, elephant tails, whales' teeth, beetles' legs, iron bars, and bits of tufted string made from the fur of a fruit-eating bat.

Our own money seems to be somewhat more sensibly based, and has its origins in such age-old objects of desire as gold, silver, women and cows. The words "capital" and "chattel" are derived from the same word as "cattle." Our "pecuniary" interests were once vested in *pecus*, the Latin term for cows. Today's "fee" stems from the Old Norse *fē*, meaning cattle, and our modern coins have "heads" and "tails."

Copper ingots found in a Bronze Age palace on the island of Crete are in the shape of oxhides, and the Homeric Greeks computed prices in terms of the ox standard. As the prize for a wrestling match, Achilles offered the winner "a large tripod to stand on the fire, which the spectators valued at twelve oxen. For the loser, he brought out a woman well skilled in women's work, valued at four oxen."

"Hard was the struggle for that fine tripod," Homer reports in the *Iliad*, leaving posterity to infer that the woman was no bargain, even at four oxen. And no wonder. Shopping around in the *Odyssey*, we learn that twenty oxen was the going price for a really first-class slave girl, for such was the price Laertes paid for Euryclea "when she was in her first youth."

While the early Greeks computed the price of slave girls in terms of cattle currency, the ancient Irish figured the price of cattle, chariots and everything else in terms of slave girls, or *kumals*. According to the *Tain*, the oldest epic poem in Western literature, the Brown Bull of Cuailnge was purchased for a chariot "worth three times seven bondsmaids." Included in the Irish King of Leinster's tax to Rome in 106 A.D. were 150 *kumals*, 150 cows, 150 swine and the king's daughter—which not only reduced the hapless monarch's capital assets but left him with one less dependent to claim for the year 107.

Though gold and silver ornaments were often used as money, the *kumal* was so popular a currency that she was considered both legal and tender as late as the Middle Ages. Easily the liveliest loot of all time, the *kumal* was valued at three cows, with sheep, heifers and bags of grain serving as small change.

Grain was also a common currency in the agrarian economy of ancient Egypt. Taxes were paid in cereals, and granaries served as banks, on which the privileged and the wealthy could draw checks against their grain deposits. Gold was mined mainly for export, and was measured in "grains" that corresponded to the weight of a grain of wheat, just as it was later measured in "carats" to the weight of a carat seed.

In similar manner, the Babylonian *shekel* was 180 grains of barley, and offered a uniform standard by which to weigh a lump of silver in 3000 B.C. Though the Lydians are generally credited with minting the first small coins in the seventh century B.C., the earlier Babylonians issued silver ingots stamped with the images of gods, who supposedly guaranteed the weight and purity of the metal. Gold and silver were stored in temples, where they would receive divine protection, and in Judea, Greece and Rome coins were minted in temples. The words "money" and "mint" are but borrowings from the Latin *Moneta*, "a surname of Juno, in whose temple at Rome money was coined."

No one seems to be certain why Juno's temple was chosen to serve as the Roman mint, but a theory might be based on the fact that she was the protectress of cattle and women—both chattels and tokens of wealth. In Greece and early Rome, upper-class wives and consorts vied for the honor of posing for the goddesses depicted on coins, but the first woman to appear as herself was Cleopatra. Judging from her profile on the silver *tetradrachma*, the Siren of the Nile would have made a dubious booby prize for a Greek wrestling match. Alexander, the first male monarch to be immortalized on money, looks just Great, however, despite the fact that he had been dead for almost a year when the coin was minted.

Ptolemy I of Egypt was the first living ruler to put his own face on a coin, but the despot with the greatest affection for his own portrait was Nero, who used Roman coins as though they were publicity photos. On one series we find Nero the Warrior. Another hails Nero the lyre-strumming Singer and Actor. On still another, Nero the speed-demon Charioteer appears with his hair crimped in the style of a hot-shot circus driver. Then came Nero the Man of Peace, followed by Nero the Ruler Who Rebuilt Rome after the famous fire.

Under pretense of making the coinage more durable, Nero reduced its silver content by 10 per cent, and pocketed the profit to support his expensive tastes. Future emperors continued the process of debasement until the proportion of pure silver was less than 2 per cent. The costs of Roman high life soared. The infamous Emperor Caracalla ran through his entire inheritance in one day, and the teen-age tyrant Heliogabalus spent close to half a million dollars on one orgiastic feast. The depleted Roman treasury issued thinly plated coins, so valueless they had to be traded by the sackful, and the army was given salt in lieu of its traditional "salt money," or *salarium*—from whence cometh our "salary."

As Rome quietly crumbled, prudent men-of-affairs retreated to remote castles with such precious metals as they could hoard, gathering their retainers about them in anticipation of the feudal period to come. Byzantium prospered with Rome's decline, and Constantine issued a solid gold *solidus* to his troops, who became so identified with the coin that later generations of military men were called "soldiers."

In Britain, Gaul and Scandinavia cattle still comprised a currency that even a Caesar couldn't counterfeit. The wily barbarians, never too impressed by coinage, preferred to deal in metals by weight. The Norsemen used a cow's ear, or *ore*, as a standard for weighing rings and coins, which they treated as bulk metal. The Roman *libra pondo*, or pound, was the unit of weight used by the British, and £, for *libra*, still serves as the symbol for the English pound note. The shilling was a *scilling*, or "a piece cut off" and tossed into the scales, while a coin was a *cuneus*, or wedge, cut from a piece of metal money as a means of making change.

Among the earliest British coins were silver pennies minted during the hesitant reign of Ethelred the Unready, who used them to buy off the marauding Vikings. These coins were known by the Latin name of *denarii*, and *d.* still stands for pence in British currency. Crude by machine-age standards, the hand-stamped coins of the Middle Ages were seldom perfectly round. Irregular shapes were expected, and the unscrupulous were able to clip and file the edges of coins and assemble hoards of silver. Though a culprit, when caught, had his right hand cut off in punishment, clipping became a favorite medieval hobby. By the 1300's money metal was so scarce that kings were forced to borrow from Italian bankers, who charged an interest of 260 per cent.

For many years Italian bankers charged no interest at all on domestic loans to merchants, but penalties for failing to keep a due date were so high that debtors often announced that they were "bench-broken," or bankrupt. As Voltaire explained it, "Every merchant had his bench (*banco*) in the place of exchange; and when he had conducted his business badly, declared himself *fallito*, and abandoned his property to his creditors with the proviso that he retain a good part of it for himself . . . There was nothing to be said to him, and his bench was broken, *banco rotto, banca rotta;* he could even, in certain towns, keep all his property and baulk his creditors, provided he seated himself bare-bottomed on a stone in the presence of all the merchants. This was a mild deviation of the old Roman proverb . . . to pay either with one's money or one's skin."

Kings were not inclined to seek relief from debt by

public display of the royal posterior, however. Threatened with financial embarrassment, Henry VIII took his cue from the Romans and slyly issued silver-plated shillings. The coins, on which the much-married monarch was depicted in full face, were mostly copper, and constant circulation soon wore the plating off Henry's proud proboscis, earning him the unregal nickname of "Old Coppernose."

During the reign of Henry's daughter Elizabeth, England's coins were once again restored to proper weight and value. With the rise of the merchant class and the growing sophistication of the cities, the common man's interest in currency increased by leaps and pounds sterling. "Get money; still get money, boy," Ben Jonson urged, while Shakespeare reflected an English attitude as well as a Paduan when he observed that the worldly-wise Petruchio would willingly marry "an old trot with ne'er a tooth in her head, though she have as many diseases as two and fifty horses," providing she had money.

In 1663 the Guinea coast of Africa provided the gold for a new coin that was logically called a "guinea." But European money was of little help to the adventurers and trading companies that began to exploit the Dark Continent for its ivory, slaves and precious metals. Even today, cattle, camels, sheep and goats are primary stores of wealth among many African tribes and currency is based on a cattle standard similar to that of the ancient Greeks.

Like most primitive peoples, the cattle-keeping Africans originally had but two uses for money: to pay a debt of "blood money" to the relatives of one's victims and to purchase wives. A girl in the medium-price range went for three cows and a bull, though most fathers were open to any reasonable deal and prices were scaled to the year and model. Since no clear distinctions were made between women and cattle, a man who preferred girls to cows could invest his wealth in wives and count himself fairly successful when he had between six and ten. As late as January, 1964, in fact, a Masai chief who was impressed with actress Carroll Baker's efforts to understand tribal ways offered to buy the blond movie star for 150 cows, 200 goats and sheep and $750 in cash —a princely price considering that Masai maidens were currently valued at only $200 and 12 cows.

The profit motive in marriage has seldom been more blatantly expressed than among the Batetela of Equatorial Africa, whose currency was copper rods. The young man opened negotiations with a simple declaration of love. The girl then replied, "All right, bring the money," and the traditional down-payment was made: a dog and eight copper rods, followed by later payments of more dogs, more rods, and chickens. Since installments often lagged over a long period of time, a favorite local taunt was that a man still owed for his grandmother.

The chief Slave Coast currency used by early Portuguese and Spanish traders was the copper or brass *manilla*—a round bar bent in the general shape of a horseshoe. But the most universally accepted metal was iron, which the natives used to make weapons and tools. These hand-fashioned implements passed as currency and in time became nonfunctional tokens. Iron hoes evolved into thin, twisted bars with flattened ends and became the "Kissi Pennies" of Sierra Leone and Liberia. Axes, spears and lethal throwing knives lost their cutting edges and degenerated into harmless currency, which scholars compare to the mysteriously nonfunctional swords and axes that have been found in the prehistoric barrows of Britain and the Continent.

Mysterious, too, are the origins of African mosaic trade beads, which the natives believe grew out of the ground. But beads, copper and iron were minor currencies compared to cowrie shells—the most widely distributed money the world has ever known. These small, tiger-striped shells were familiar to Phoenician traders and are believed to have been used as Roman fertility symbols. Vaginal in appearance, and impossible to counterfeit, cowries were standard currency in Africa, India, the Pacific Islands and ancient China. Chinese word characters for "riches," "prices," "buying" and "selling" all contain the early symbol for "shell," and cowries were in daily use until the close of the second century B.C., when the first Sublime Emperor outlawed them in favor of round brass coins with square holes in the center.

Since Chinese coins were cast rather than stamped, counterfeiting was easy, and 100,000 forgers were nabbed in one year alone. Hoping to foil the free-lance money artists, Wang Mang the Usurper called in all existing currency in 10 A.D. and issued a whole new set of coins, valued as Wee, Small, Young, Next, Almost, Middle, Mature, Approximate, Second-best and Largest. When even this failed, Wang sought to abandon all metal currency and bring back the more reliable cowrie

—a remarkably sensible reform, for which he was quite naturally murdered.

Because of the cowrie's inherent soundness, Africans usually preferred the shell to European coins. The first coin that really caught the native fancy was the Austrian *taler* of 1780, which bore the bosomy portrait of the Empress Maria Theresa. The demand for this silver coin was so great that it was reissued throughout the nineteenth century, and the British Royal Mint had to strike off several hundred thousand for trade purposes in the years between 1936 and 1962—all with Maria Theresa's bust and all dated 1780.

Coins bearing the well-upholstered image of Queen Victoria were also highly regarded, though her currency was no longer accepted after her death. According to native belief, when the Queen died, her money died too and was therefore without value. A notable exception existed in Tibet, however, where the Queen's crown was mistaken for the headgear of a mendicant Buddhist monk and Victoria was known as the Vagabond Lama.

Crowns and queenly bosoms notwithstanding, coins of any sort were lackluster loot compared to the exotic currencies traders encountered in the Pacific. In Borneo, for example, currency was based on old brass cannons. Values were established in terms of imaginary units of cannon, known as *pikuls,* which were applied to such routine mediums of exchange as buffaloes, beeswax and brass gongs.

Farther south, on the tiny Island of Alor, a more complex system was founded on the natives' single-minded devotion to the accumulation and investment of gongs, drums and pigs. The gongs were seldom struck, the drums were never played, and the pigs were roasted and eaten only at feasts—which were usually scheduled to coincide with the death of a pig. Borrowing and lending drums and gongs were the sole male occupations, while the women provided for food and shelter. Since a feast was the only occasion when a man could be forced to pay his debts, it was considered sound business practice for a creditor to shoot a debtor's pig and force him to give a feast. Drums and gongs were spent only for the purchase of wives or pigs.

The same sort of bills were paid with dogs' teeth in the Admiralty Islands, while strings of shells and arm rings procured a young girl-mate in Bougainville. "Buy me with arm rings," the native siren sang to her lover; and an old Melanesian ballad has the boy giving a familiar blues treatment to such lyrics as these:

If you did not want me,
Why did you tell me to give you a string of red shell money?
Your father demanded two hundred fathoms of red shell money;
That was your price,
You unwashed old scarecrow.
You are as old as an opossum.

In equally romantic New Britain the bride price was roughly that of a used canoe, payable in shells. In other parts of the polygamous Pacific wives were bought and magicians' fees were paid with boars' tusks, hand-woven mats, small feathers plucked from around the eyes of fowls, flying-fox fur, and disks of polished turtle shell that bore the remorseful-sounding name of *alas*.

The Pacific is also the home of the biggest money in the world—the Great Stone Money of the Island of Yap. The larger denominations of this cumbersome currency stand twelve feet high, weigh over a ton and are cut in the shape of huge millstones. A hole in the center permits the native Yappers to trundle the smaller pieces of change around by means of stout wooden axles, but the really big money is kept on display outside the houses of the original owners. Title to a stone may be transferred by means of an inscription, and physical possession is not essential to ownership. One family traded for years on the hidden value of a huge wheel that had sunk into the sea while being transported from a Palau stone quarry four hundred miles away.

In the Palaus, where it is abundant, the stone holds no monetary interest for the natives, who are too busy keeping track of their *kluks*, *adeloboks* and other bead moneys, which come in more denominations than any other currency on earth. Both the Yappers and the Palau Islanders were inclined to view each other's currency with tolerant amusement until the United States Navy came along with the funniest money either had ever seen —paper!

Considering that they had already learned to mistrust the trade coinage of Spain, Germany and Japan, the islanders accepted our World War II military dollars with commendable faith—far more, in fact, than Americans themselves displayed when the Continental Congress issued its paper currency in 1775. Despite threats of imprisonment and "loss of both ears," the sons and daughters of the Revolution valiantly refused to honor the scrip, and "not worth a Continental" became a folk phrase for worthlessness.

But money troubles were nothing new in the thirteen original colonies. The first New England settlers had landed on Plymouth Rock with less cash than Junior takes away to camp. High in hopes and low in funds, the Pilgrims made out as best they could by bartering corn, musket bullets and fish.

Contrary to popular belief, it was the pence-poor Pilgrims who introduced wampum to the local Indians, who had never seen bead money before. The first strings were purchased from a Dutch ship's captain, who had learned of their uses while trafficking with tribes along the Hudson River. Though the polished shell beads bore a disturbing resemblance to sinful ornaments, the Pilgrims tried them out on the Indians, who eagerly bought them in exchange for beaver skins that could be sold in England.

Because of tight money conditions in England, only a trickle of British currency circulated in the colonies. Minting was prohibited in America by royal edict, and the settlers took such coins as they could get: Dutch *guilders*, Swedish *dalers*, French *louis*, and silver pieces of eight from Spanish mints in Mexico. It's from the use of Spanish coins that we get our oldest American money term, "two bits," which dates back to the early settlers. "Bit" was the English name for the Spanish *reale*, or one eighth of a piece of eight. "Two bits" was a fourth of this popular silver dollar and quite properly came to apply to our quarter.

The first American coins worthy of the name were Willow-Tree shillings, which, along with Oak- and Pine-Tree shillings, were minted without royal permission in 1652. But it wasn't until after the Revolution that Americans began to coin money on a wholesale basis. Under the Articles of Confederation coinage powers were granted to the States, which, in turn, granted minting patents to individuals. A man named Mould made copper pennies for New Jersey. Ephraim Brasher issued his own doubloons in New York, where even the John Street Theatre circulated its own privately minted pennies. Citizens of the little community of Castorland, N.Y., proudly flipped Paris-made half dollars bearing the thunderous motto, "Hail, Thou Mighty Mother of Production," while the Federal Congress authorized the minting of copper cents featuring a sundial symbol of Time. "I Fly," Time prudently warned. "Mind Your Business."

In the heady atmosphere of freshly won freedom, minting and counterfeiting proceeded apace until the Constitution was ratified, reserving all powers of coinage to the Federal government. At Alexander Hamilton's suggestion a dollar "unit" based on the Spanish peso was adopted, but the United States Mint didn't start coining money until 1792. Situated on the site of an old distillery in Philadelphia, the Mint opened with a stock of six pounds of used copper and melted down some of George Washington's table silver to strike off a handful of "half-dismes," which were presented to Martha Washington—possibly in memory of her forks and spoons.

"There has also been a small beginning in the coinage of half-dismes," Washington was able to report at the next session of Congress, "the want of small coins calling first attention to them."

With the Mint slowly stamping out coppers and dimes, the need for all sorts of currency grew increasingly critical. During the next sixty years, Congress repeatedly threatened to shut down the whole minting operation and continued to sanction the use of foreign coins as legal tender. Trade was conducted largely with Spanish dollars, and accounts were kept in a confusion of pesos, shillings and pence. The dollar sign, $, is supposed to have evolved from a bookkeepers' shorthand version of PS for peso, and the American dollar was hardly more than a theoretical unit used to evaluate other currency, much as Borneo's *pikuls* of brass cannon were used to evaluate beeswax and gongs.

During the War of 1812, all coin payments were suspended and banks issued paper currency that was limited only by the availability of printing presses and the supply of ink. Private banks with wilderness addresses sprung up in the West and issued "wildcat" notes. In Michigan, where banks were required to back their paper currency with 30 per cent in specie, the same bags of coin were hustled from bank to bank, one step ahead of the inspectors. As one official described it: "Gold and silver flew about the country with the celerity of magic; its sound was heard in the depths of the forest, yet like the wind, one knew not whence it came or whither it was going."

In 1834 a "hard money" bloc in Congress pushed for a reform measure that favored a gold dollar. A new mint that operated on live horsepower was set up two years later, and with the discovery of gold in California the production of gold coins increased to the point where the minting of cents and dimes fell off and no one had any change. After discussing the crisis for two years, Congress swung into action and authorized a new series of coins in the now-familiar five-to-fifty-cent denominations. The Mint worked on a twenty-four-hour schedule, new coins poured into circulation, and America had enough currency to cover its needs for the first time in history.

Pockets jingled but briefly, however. With the outbreak of the Civil War, coin metal became so scarce that paper greenbacks were declared legal tender. In addition to Federal notes, 7,000 different bank issues were in circulation, together with 5,000 odd lots of passable counterfeits. It has been estimated that before the war ended one third of the money in the country was counterfeit, and in the final days of the Confederacy bogus bills bearing the names of Northern banks were more negotiable than the South's legal but low-value "shinplasters." Out of this near-catastrophic muddle the legislation essential to a sound national currency was born.

Vital as these matters are to our present security, schoolroom emphasis upon the details of the currency and banking reforms of the period has left many present-day Americans with the impression that the history of money is a tedious compendium of boring dates and technicalities. At the time, however, American money views were often quite emotional. As a result of William Jennings Bryan's passionate advocacy of Free Silver and the common man's sentimental support of the underdog metal, Government officials complained in 1960 that 35,000,000, unused silver dollars were creating a serious storage problem for the Denver Mint. Only 400,000 were in circulation—mostly in Las Vegas, where they were fed into slot machines; in Alaska; and in parts of Texas (where, it was sometimes alleged, they served as nickels and dimes). Nevada, scene of the big nineteenth-century silver diggings, had always been partial to the outsize coins. When the Comstock lode was struck, the bullion-happy citizens sang:

Oh, give me a silver dollar
I can lay on the bar with a bang.
Money that folds may do for the East,
But we want our dollars to clang!

In the interests of convenience and good posture, the majority of Americans have traditionally avoided the weighty cartwheels and derived their audio satisfactions from crisp new bills that snap, crackle and pop. Apathy toward the silver dollar has been so pronounced that when a bank in Santa Monica, California, ran a Dollar Day sale in 1961, at which silver dollars were offered at ninety-eight cents apiece, few people cared to take advantage of the bargain and the bank reported "business as usual."

As late as 1946, however, Congress enacted laws requiring the Federal Government to support the market price of silver by buying all that was offered at ninety and one-half cents an ounce and selling it when needed by industrial users at ninety-one cents. In the fall of 1961 the Treasury had some 1,700,000,000 ounces of silver in its stockpile, all but 22,000,000, of which were needed to back the nation's one-, two-, five- and ten-dollar silver certificates. In recent years industry's increasing demand for the silver bullion needed to manufacture tableware, photographic film, missile components and atomic submarine batteries had outstripped the annual output of American producers—a situation that would have caused silver prices to rise, were it not for the fact that the metal was still available from the Government stockpile at a low ninety-one cents an ounce. Silver producers, who had been dependent upon Federal stockpiling and price support when the industrial demand was weak, now urged the Treasury to raise its sales price or stop selling silver to industry. When, in November, 1961, the Government's supply of purchasable bulk silver had dwindled to the point where it would have been entirely depleted in three weeks' time, President Kennedy ordered the Treasury to stop selling silver to industry and prepared to ask Congress to repeal the Silver Purchase Acts—a move necessary to take the Government out of the silver market for all time.

With a view to eliminating the need for a Federal stockpile, the Treasury was further directed to draw the silver needed for minting coins from the reserves on hand—including the portion that provided dollar-for-dollar backing for American silver certificates. While the Treasury would continue to honor such certificates, the long-range plan was to retire the silver-backed currency in favor of Federal Reserve notes backed by a combination of 25 per cent in Government-held gold and 75 per cent in the assets of the issuing Reserve banks. As a result of the new open market in silver, prices rose to $1.19 a troy ounce by September, 1962, and to $1.28 an ounce in March of the following year. As the market price mounted, interest in silver dollars grew and money specialists speculated that the day might come when the seventy-seven hundredths of an ounce of silver in each coin might be worth more than a dollar, thus making it profitable for Americans to melt the old cartwheels down into bulk metal and sell the metal to industry.

According to Secretary of the Treasury Douglas Dillon, the smelting of silver coinage would become profitable when the price of bulk silver reached $1.38 an ounce. But many silver dollars were already worth much more than that as collectors' items, some rare specimens having been valued as high as $2,000. None had been minted since 1935, and coin dealers' prices continued to advance with the phenomenal growth of numismatics as an American hobby. With interest in silver dollars at an all-time peak, unprecedented numbers of the hefty coins were being removed from circulation by the nation's 8,000,000 hobbyists and an undetermined number of speculators and hoarders. Aware of the rapidly diminishing supply, the Bureau of the Mint applied to Congress in 1963 for the funds necessary to resume minting dollars. Though it seemed likely that the silver content of the new coins would undoubtedly have to be reduced to prevent profitable smelting in the foreseeable future, cartwheel fanciers were cheered by the hope that the proposed new minting would prevent the American dollar from becoming a mere unit of Federal paper.

Following the assassination of President Kennedy, rumors circulated that the new dollars would memorialize the President's death. Congress, however, at President Johnson's suggestion, authorized a Kennedy fifty-cent piece, and when the proposal to mint new dollars was rejected in the closing days of March, 1964, long lines of collectors, dealers, speculators and ordinary citizens formed outside the Treasury building in Washington to redeem their silver certificates for silver dollars. Stimulated by word that the Treasury's inventory included a number of valuable specimens designed by George T. Morgan and minted between 1878 and 1921, some collectors brought boxes, laundry bags and toy express wagons to haul away their ponderous treasures. As lines grew longer, the original limit of one $50,000 transaction per person was reduced to $1,000 and certificates could be traded for silver dollars only between the hours of nine and eleven A.M. But the Government supply still quickly shrank to a meager 3,000,000, coins—at which point the Treasury halted sales, since no means could be found for their equitable distribution. As an alternative, the Treasury offered to redeem outstanding silver certificates in silver bullion on the following day, but only $113 was turned in for packets of the dull-gray metal crystals. Americans, it seemed, were not interested in silver for silver's sake. However belatedly, they had merely come to value, respect and admire a silver dollar that clanged.

In the months following the "silver-dollar rush," an

increasing number of the now-desirable coins were taken out of circulation by collectors, souvenir hunters, hoarders and speculators. The size of some individual holdings was indicated in June of 1964, when a leading numismatic journal carried an ad offering a ton of "bright uncirculated" dollars for $39,995—a price that was nearly $7,000 in excess of the face value of the coin. In Western states, meanwhile, the shortage of circulating silver dollars became a major political issue, and Senators and Representatives urged Congress to pass a $600,000 measure that would permit the Denver Mint to strike off 45,000,000 new dollar coins. The measure was finally passed in mid-summer, despite the opposition of those Congressmen and money specialists who felt that all mint facilities should be concentrated on producing coins of smaller denominations, which were in equally critical short supply.

Throughout the early 1960's the increase of coin-gobbling vending machines, parking meters, tolls, sales taxes, piggy banks and private coin collections had led to recurring shortages of pennies, nickels, dimes and quarters. In the spring of 1964, the New York *Times* reported that the scarcity of coins had become "an acute problem for retail business." In one June week, New York's First National City Bank had only $300 in pennies to meet the needs of its 126 branches. A leading lunch-counter chain offered free coffee to bus and taxi drivers who were willing to exchange their small coins for paper bills. Other retailers solicited local churches in the devout hope of acquiring the coins dropped in Sunday collection plates and poor-boxes. In July, "Sorry—No Change" signs began to appear in Chicago. A bank in Beloit, Wisconsin, offered ten trading stamps for each dollar's-worth of change received, with an extra ten-stamp bonus for each roll of nickels. When the coin shortage hit Nantucket Island at the height of the summer tourist season, an enterprising gift-shop proprietor emulated his Yankee predecessors and issued his own commercially-minted coins in "two-bit" and "four-bit" denominations. Slightly larger than our regular quarters and fifty-cent pieces, the aluminum coins bore the portrait of a smiling whale, and were soon circulating all over the island as "Whale Money," redeemable for legal U.S. tender upon demand at the gift shop.

Coin shortage or no, some question existed as to the legality of the old whaling port's aluminum money, since only the Federal Government has the power to issue coinage. Amidst persistent rumors that the Treasury itself planned to issue metal coins with a reduced or nonexistent silver content, the Federal minting operation was put on a twenty-four-hour basis in an effort to double its output and bypass the coin crisis by early 1965. Production details were streamlined, new stamping machines were put into operation, and the date on all new coins was frozen to read "1964" for an indefinite period to come—a dodge designed to make the new coins less interesting to coin collectors, who sadly envisioned the day when the dating on American coins would become as fictitious and meaningless as that on the old Maria Theresa trade dollars. The cost of this round-the-clock minting program was estimated at $10,000,000, though the Treasury stood to make double, or even triple, that amount from the sale of the new coins. These included our copper pennies, which are partly tin; our nickels, which are mostly copper; and silver dimes, quarters and half-dollars, which—oddly enough, in light of the Treasury's rapidly dwindling supply—are still mostly silver.

The metallic value of all these coins is considerably less than their face value. A mere twelve cents' worth of metal is required to make a dollars' worth of nickels, for instance, and Treasury officials have estimated the annual profit from minting to be in the vicinity of $55,000,000. At least part of the profit is attributable to a law that makes it illegal to change the design of a given coin more than once every twenty-five years. In addition, the Mint's outlay for models' fees has been practically nil. Legend has it that when the eagle was selected as our national emblem the Philadelphia Mint adopted a live specimen named Peter, who posed for several early coins before he got tangled up in the Mint's machinery. Peter died as a result of his injuries, but he retained his Civil Service status through the thoughtfulness of fellow employees who had the bald bird stuffed.

Though the Mint was not on a first-name basis with the bison who posed for the buffalo nickel, the Indian was long thought to be a chap named Two Guns Whitecalf. According to designer James Earle Fraser, however, the portrait was a composite of three other braves —Irontail, Two Moons, and a taciturn type with long braids who never did give his name.

The Indian on the old penny was a pale-faced squaw named Sarah Longacre, daughter of a Mint official, while the Lincoln, Washington, Jefferson, Franklin, Roosevelt and Kennedy coins were all done from portraits. When designer John Sinnock added his initials to the Roosevelt dime in 1946, word spread among the benighted that the tiny "J.S." stood for Joseph Stalin and was the work of subversives boring from within the Mint. Assigned to design the Franklin half dollar in 1948, Sinnock therefore took the precaution of adding his middle initial, "R." This touched off a new rumor: the Mint's subversives had become so entrenched that they were boldly defacing our coinage with Stalin's middle name. History, ever prone to attacks of hysteria, repeated itself once again in April, 1964, when the appearance of the Kennedy half dollar brought complaints to the Denver Mint that the coin bore a Communist hammer and sickle. "It's my monogram," Chief Sculptor and Engraver Gilroy Roberts explained, "a G. and an R. in script, combined. It might look like two sickles maybe. But it looks nothing like a hammer and sickle at all. You've got to have a slanted mind to see that there."

As might be expected, the intrinsic value of paper money is even less than that of coin. It costs approximately $10 to run off 1,000 bills, whether their face value is $1 or $10,000, and changes in design are much less frequent. The biggest change in the appearance of American paper money was its reduction in size in 1929. A less obvious but more momentous change occurred in 1933-34, when the dollar went off the gold standard and paper currency was no longer redeemable in gold coin.

To venture even a summary of the significance of this change is to become involved in a maelstrom of economic theories. Reading the fine print on the engravings in our billfold, however, we find that a ten-dollar Federal Reserve note is "legal tender for all debts public and private, and is redeemable in lawful money at the United States Treasury, or at any Federal Reserve Bank." The large type, above and below Jefferson's portrait, billboards the comforting guarantee that "The United States of America will pay to the bearer on demand Ten Dollars." In terms of our daily money operations this means that a ten-dollar bill will get you two paper fives or a clutch of ten paper ones—which, since the advent of our new one-dollar Federal Reserve notes, are no longer redeemable for any coin or coins with a near-dollar's worth of intrinsic value.

It would appear, then, that we are presently trading in government tokens similar to the debased coinage of Imperial Rome and the Continental paper of Revolutionary America. But, actually, no such comparisons can be made. Our modern currency does not pretend to derive its value from the amount it represents in static metal. It is based, rather, on the purchasing power of a "commodity dollar" and is more realistically rooted in the nation's capacity to produce and reproduce a wealth of goods and services—a concept that often seems nebulous to minds still operating on the gold standard, but one that would be beautifully clear to the earlier herdsmen, whose cattle wealth reproduced itself time and again through the ages.

But, we recall, it is gold ingots and not "commodity dollars" that the Government keeps locked up in the vault at Fort Knox, Ky. Surely this would seem to suggest that old-fashioned gold has some uses beyond that of making dental inlays. And it does. Though the huge pile of glittering bricks stored in the mausoleum at the corner of Dixie Highway and Bullion Boulevard may seem as remote from our personal money transactions as a twelve-foot stone on the Island of Yap, it is essential to the prestige and support of the American dollar abroad. Gold is still the international medium of exchange and is needed to cover those situations where American goods and services will not suffice.

Up to and including the year 1963, the export of American goods and services has continued to exceed her imports by a healthy margin, and from the standpoint of trade America has regularly earned more gold than she has been required to spend for imported raw materials and products. Unfortunately, however, the profits made in trade are more than canceled out by our expenditures for overseas defense and economic aid to needy (and, hopefully, friendly) nations. Since 1949, in fact, the combined total of American commitments, investments and purchases abroad has exceeded our foreign-trade profits in all years but one—1957—and has diminished our national gold reserves at the average rate of about 600 million dollars a year.

To a greater or lesser extent, this imbalance shows every sign of continuing as part of America's price for leadership of the free world. Paradoxically at times, the amount of American gold payments has caused world confidence in the dollar to waver. The problem of stemming the drain on our gold reserves has, therefore, been a major subject for concern among our government leaders, bankers, economists—and, of late, the general public, whose newspapers and magazines have created a vivid and alarming picture of the "flight" of gold from our shores.

In reality, very little of the gold needed to cover our deficits abroad actually leaves the country. For the most part, such payments are made from a cache of Treasury bullion held in the United States Assay Office in New York City and involve a short six-block trip by armored car to the New York Federal Reserve Bank, where the ingots owed are simply stacked in the various piles allocated to foreign governments and banks. Despite the size and frequency of recent payments, moreover, the United States still owns more gold than any other nation on earth—though an unknown, and admittedly sizable, reserve has been building up in the Soviet Union. Unlike most of the world's gold, which includes metal mined by the ancient Egyptians, Soviet bullion is largely new, and has been blasted and dug from the ore-rich Siberian tundra in a mining effort that has reportedly involved a labor force of half a million. In the past decade whole cities have sprung up in the Russian gold fields and increasing mechanization has resulted in a production rate which has been estimated to be at least three times that of the United States.

To what purpose have the Soviets initiated this twentieth-century gold rush? The Russians themselves are most guarded in their replies. When the subject of gold was broached during former Premier Khrushchev's visit to France in March, 1960, he playfully begged the question. "Gold we have, but we save it. Why? I don't really know. Lenin said the day would come when gold would serve to coat the walls and floors of public toilets. When the Communist society is built, we must certainly accomplish Lenin's wish."

No one was so naïve as to believe that the Soviets were hoarding gold for the purpose of beautifying municipal rest rooms, however. Since Khrushchev's coy demurral in 1960, the Russians have repeatedly demonstrated their ability to use gold for the fulfillment of the Communist purpose. Like the United States, the Soviet Union has used its bullion to cover foreign deficits and establish credit with the West. In the fall of 1963, literally tons upon tons of Russian gold were dumped on European markets to raise the cash needed to pay for Soviet purchases of Western wheat. This sudden dumping had the effect of lowering the European demand for American gold payments and temporarily strengthened our position. But the thought occurs that if the Soviets were given the opportunity to sell and withhold such massive accumulations of gold regularly, as part of a long-term economic strategy, the result might just as easily prove disastrous to the whole free world.

In an all-out economic cold war it would seem that the strategic use of gold could be every bit as decisive as the strategic use of nuclear weapons in a war that was military and hot. Indeed, the stockpiling of both gold and weapons invites the speculation that bombs and bullion may be more alike than we had reason to suspect. In view of this similarity and previously noted instances of weapons' evolving into harmless currency, the student of money is prompted to offer the suggestion that a nuclear war might well be averted by simply switching the international monetary base from gold to H-bombs. Since nations are notably reluctant to part with their monetary treasures, the new nuclear wealth would be considered too precious to waste in waging war. It would be kept in vaults and cherished, as gold is cherished today, while money values might be measured in *pikuls* of nonfunctional H-bombs, redeemable for the joys of peace.

The more immediate question, though, is not whether dollars and rubles will ever be based on a nuclear standard but whether the whole idea of money might not be on the way out. With the growing popularity of credit cards and the advent of automated accounting, some have foreseen the possibility that currency will gradually be replaced by one vast system of credit. But the men who know money best are still far from alarmed, and currency buffs stoutly insist that money will never die. As one veteran mazuma hunter put it in an interview, conducted outside the loan department of a large Manhattan bank: "Lissen, if anybody seriously thinks that money is going out of style, all he has to do to get straightened out quick is to take Benjamin Franklin's advice and just try to *borrow* some!"

II

SHAVES AND HAIRCUTS

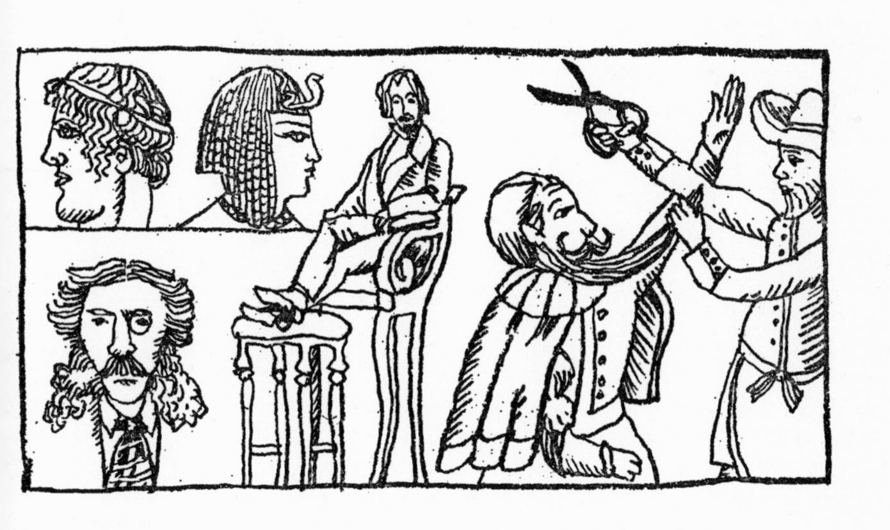

Shaves and Haircuts

Among the many goods and services for which mankind has spent untold billions of dollars, pounds, pesos, *pikuls* and cowrie shells are those connected with the care, cultivation and conservation of that most curious of all human growths: the hair. People were fiddling with their hair long before the invention of money, and at various times and places the filaments of Man's face and scalp have been cut, shaved, plucked, curled, singed, braided, dyed, bleached, waxed, waved, oiled, greased, powdered, plastered, combed, brushed, fondled, fetished, feared, envied and adored.

According to the bewhiskered psychologist, Havelock

Ellis, hair is "the most generally noted part of the feminine body after the eyes." Judging from the cartoonists' conception of primitive courting behavior, it was also the most frequently grabbed, and Stone Age beauties were continually being dragged off on dates by shaggy clubmen, who towed them along by the tresses.

Actually, however, many primitive peoples believe that the head and all its hairs are occupied by spirits and are taboo to the touch. In *The Golden Bough*, Sir James George Frazer's masterwork on myths, folklore and religion, the anthropologist records that if a Maori so much as scratched his head with his fingers, "he was immediately obliged to apply them to his nose, and snuff up the sanctity which they had acquired by the touch," and that the son of a Marquesan high priest "has been seen to roll on the ground in an agony of rage and despair, begging for death, because someone had desecrated his head and deprived him of his divinity by sprinkling a few drops of water on his hair."

Among such taboo-ridden types there is no such thing as a once-over-lightly, Frazer notes, and "when it becomes necessary to crop the hair, measures are taken to lessen the dangers which are supposed to attend the operation. The chief of Namosi in Fiji always ate a man by way of precaution when he had his hair cut. . . . Amongst the Maoris many spells were uttered at hair-cutting; one, for example, was spoken to consecrate the obsidian knife with which the hair was cut; another was pronounced to avert the thunder and lightning which hair-cutting was believed to cause."

The notion that hair is a source of supernatural power

is common to most ancient religions and is reflected in the Biblical law of Leviticus, which requires that men "shall not make baldness upon their head, neither shall they shave off the corner of their beard." To cut a man's hair or beard against his will was to offer him the greatest indignity, and when the minions of Hanun sent David's good-will ambassadors packing, they first "shaved off one half of their beards and cut off their garments in the middle, even unto their buttocks." David, it will be recalled, was not half so affronted by their bare backsides as he was by the brevity of their whiskers, and he sent messengers to head them off with an order to "Tarry at Jericho until your beards be grown."

The most famous haircut of all time, of course, was the Old Testament trimming Delilah gave Samson at the behest of the scheming Philistines. Having wheedled the Scriptural strong man into revealing that the source of all his strength lay in his hair, "she made him sleep upon her knees; and she called for a man, and she caused him to shave off the seven locks of his head . . . and his strength went from him." In time the hair grew in again and Samson avenged the cause of all embattled longhairs by toppling the Philistines' house, bringing the roof down on their heads.

Like most ancient peoples, the Hebrews cut their hair and beards only at times of penitence and bereavement. The Egyptians, on the other hand, regularly shaved their heads and faces and let their hair grow only when in mourning. Egyptian priests, Herodotus tells us, "shaved their whole body every other day," while the rest of the populace had their heads shaved "from early childhood . . . and so by the action of the sun the skull becomes thick and hard." For all their hardheadedness, the Egyptians were never so thickskulled as to maintain that baldness was beautiful, however. From the earliest days of the Old Kingdom wigs were worn by men and women alike.

On ceremonial occasions the clean-shaven Pharaohs wore a false beard that eventually took the form of a golden triangle. Whether of gold or hair, the beard was traditionally a symbol of virility, maturity, wisdom and authority. As such, the ample beards of the Assyrians were proudly arranged in rows of curls stiffened with perfumed gum. Curly, too, were the beards of the early Greeks, though young men usually shaved and whiskers went out of fashion with Alexander the Great, who ordered his troops to shave their faces clean on the grounds that a soldier's beard offered too convenient a handle for an enemy to seize at close quarters.

While the Greeks were not known to shave their scalps, ladies of fashion wore wigs that copied the elegant hairstyles of the *hetaerae*, the pampered class of paid courtesans. In like manner, the prostitutes of Caesar's day inspired a fad for bleached hair and blond wigs among the wives and mistresses of the Roman upper crust. Since prostitutes were required to wear yellow hair by law, it soon became evident that many men preferred blondes, and amorously inclined amateurs began to advertise their lusty proclivities by flaunting golden locks. Led by the noble nymphomaniac, Messalina, who nightly donned a blond wig to work the night shift at a public brothel, the passionate patricians set a style that swept all Rome. The demand for blond hair became so great that it had to be imported from Germany by the shipload, and hairdressers did a brisk trade in bleaching frisky brunettes.

Crude bleaches and hot curling irons made the loss of women's hair frequent enough for Ovid to protest their continued use, though he did favor the removal of unwanted body hair: "Should I warn you to keep the rank goat out of your armpits?" he beauty-hinted in *The Art of Love*. "Warn you to keep your legs free of coarse bristling hair?" Male amorists were similarly advised to stay neatly trimmed and shaved: "Don't let your hair grow long, and when you visit a barber, patronize only the best. Don't let him mangle your beard."

At a time when razors were roughhewn and dull iron scissors resembled small hedge clippers, even the best barbers were none too adept, while the majority were downright murderous. "He who desires not to go down to Stygian shades, let him, if he be wise, avoid barber Antiochus," Martial cautioned out of painful experience. "With gentler touch the surgeon Alcon cuts the knotted hernia and lops away broken bones with workman's hand."

Because of the lethal crudity of Roman razors, it was impossible for a man to shave himself, and every citizen and noble was a slave to his barber. Prices were high, and soapless shaves were painful, but each day at dawn customers congregated courageously at the established shops to await their turns on the stool. As Martial observed, a good barber proceeded so slowly that while he was "smoothing the skin, and making a second thorough clip of the close-cut hair, my barber became a bearded man himself."

Understandably, a young Roman's first shave was celebrated with a coming-of-age ceremony that marked his emergence into manhood. On this occasion, the hairs of the beard were offered to the gods in a religious rite which was eagerly anticipated by all members of the family. When, as Suetonius tells us, young Nero visited his wealthy aunt Domitia Lapida, who was "confined to bed with severe constipation," the old lady affectionately fondled the budding monster's downy beard and wistfully murmured, "Whenever you celebrate your coming-of-age ceremony and present me with this, I shall die happy." Whereupon the roguish teen-ogre "turned to his courtiers and said laughingly: 'In that case I must shave at once'—which he did. Then he ordered the doctors to give her a laxative of fatal strength, seized her property before she was quite dead," and tore up her will.

By way of late-late gossip, Suetonius repeats the rumor that young Augustus "used to soften the hair on his legs by singeing them with red-hot walnut shells" in order to make himself more alluring to his overly fond foster father, Julius Caesar, who, in turn, had "certain other hairy parts" of his own body "depilated with tweezers." More sensitive concerning his baldness than about having his pubic hairs yanked out by the roots, Julius "used to comb the thin strands forward from his poll" and made chintzy use of a laurel wreath to hide the bare spots.

Early Britons, according to Julius's firsthand account, had "long flowing hair" and shaved "every part of their bodies except the head and upper lip," from which dangled long, drooping mustaches that were often dyed blue, green or orange. Danish warriors, bulky and bold, were as hair-happy as the silky young models in a modern shampoo commercial and groomed their shoulder-length tresses as carefully as if they were going to a prom. Short hairstyles for Frankish royalty came in with Charlemagne and reached a dazzling extreme in the well-polished pate of Charles the Bald, who could take Christian comfort in St. Paul's widely preached opinion "that if a man have long hair, it is a shame unto him."

As a result of Paul's aversion to long hair, the clergy of the Roman Church had been tonsured since the seventh century. The shaved heads of monk and priest were so familiar a sight at the time of the Norman invasion of England that one of King Harold's spies, assigned to make a count of William's troops, mistook the close-cropped Normans for an army of priests sent to "chant masses." This erroneous intelligence, relayed to the English monarch, led to such a fatal misjudgment of Norman strength that William became the Conqueror.

It wasn't long, however, before the lengthy beards and draped finery of the English captured the fancy of the victorious Normans, and during the ensuing Crusades the home-grown Gothic whiskers of both were overshadowed by the fierce Moslem-type beards and mustachios of knights returning from the Middle East. Unsightly in the eyes of the Church, the exotic imports were denounced by Bishop Serle, who described the hirsute Henry I and his hairy henchmen as "filthy goats and bristly Saracens" and made so passionate a plea for Christian haircuts that both king and courtiers weepingly consented to let the pontiff scissor off their offensive fleece in the midst of mass in the parish church.

No less offensive to the pious was the erotic appeal of women's hair, the mere sight of which supposedly had the power to drive men into frenzies of lust. For this reason, head coverings and caps were worn indoors and out by women of all ages, though by Chaucer's time long hair was allowed to hang in beribboned braids, as did Emelye's in *The Knight's Tale:*

> *Hir yelow heer was brayded in a tresse*
> *Bihinde hir bak, a yerde long, I gess.*

Whether naturally blond or dyed with saffron, a head of "yelow heer" was a woman's crowning glory, and female criminals were sentenced to have their cherished tresses sheared off in public. When a London prostitute was caught soliciting off limits, she was taken to the pillory "with minstrelsye" and had her hair cut "round about her head." To the merry music of flutes and trumpets, male procurers and keepers of "leaping-houses" were given the same distinctive trims and lost their beards in the bargain. To avoid such conspicuous consequences, pimps and harlots often set up sexual speak-easies in barbershops and bathhouses, which became medieval versions of modern "massage" salons.

With an eye to eliminating the erotic "extras" which took the place of hot towels and spicy tonics in fourteenth-century barbershops, London authorities chose one Richard le Barber to make a monthly "scrutiny throughout the whole of his trade," to discover "any among them keeping brothels." Since barbers also ran the notorious baths, or "stew houses," it can be assumed that Richard's monthly tour was one long walk on the wild side. As the first Master of the Barbers' Company, he not only had to keep on the lookout for bawds behind every bush but was required to supervise the surgical side of barbery, which included bloodletting, cupping, cauterization and the pulling of teeth.

To advertise these sanguinary sidelines, the barber-surgeon hung a brass bleeding basin on a blood-red pole wrapped with white bandage and set it in front of his shop—thus planting the precedent for the present-day barber's pole. Attempts at a harder sell were discouraged by a London ordinance of 1307, which stated "that no barbers shall be so bold or so hardy as to put blood in their windows, openly or in view of folk, but let them have it privily carried unto the Thames." That the blood was often carried away by the bucketful we cannot doubt, since complaints were continually being made against bumbling barbers whose surgery left their patrons "worse off at their departure than they were at their coming; and that, by reason of the inexperience of the same barbers, such persons are oftentimes maimed." Though the hazards of getting a haircut were considerably less lethal, Edward III prudently preserved his long hair and forked beard, while other hair hobbyists cultivated beavers in the shapes of spades, stilettos, corkscrews and spreading fantails—the latter beauties being stiffened with wax or gum and protected by special nightcaps during sleep.

In the first half of the fifteenth century hair was frequently cropped above the ear in the curious soup-bowl style worn by Sir Laurence Olivier in the movie version of Shakespear's *Henry V* and by Richard Burton in *Becket.* Shaving became more popular, and Edward IV's household "Barbour" was instructed to appear "every satterday night if it please the Kinge to cleanse his head, leggs or feete, and for his shaveing." As Saturday nights continued to roll around, the throne passed from Richard Crookback to Henry VII and shoulder-length curls were sported by "ye prowd galantts," who—in the words of the eternal critic "Anonymous"—went strutting about with "long here" in their eyes, bringing England "to gret payne."

England didn't begin to know what "payne" was until the sixteenth century, however, when hair went wild in a bizarre assortment of beards and wigs. The age began mildly enough, when clean-shaven Henry VIII sealed a verbal agreement with Francis I of France by vowing to let his beard grow as long as the pact was in effect. When it became expedient to scuttle the agreement, Henry followed Nero's lead and had his beard shaved on the spot. To explain the breach of faith, Sir Thomas Boleyn was sent to tell the king of France that Henry's Queen Catherine objected to a "bushy chin." Oddly enough, it was Francis who was responsible for the later vogue for close-cropped hair, worn with pancake hats. By way of a little winter sport, the French monarch let his hair down to indulge in a snowball fight, when somebody tossed a firebrand at his head, "which grievously wounded him, and obliged the hair to be cut off." To help the clobbered king forget his smoldering loss, courtiers adopted the same regal clip with a verve that made it smart to be shorn, and the mode became universal.

In keeping with the French fashion, Henry VIII had his hair trimmed short in 1535 and balanced the loss on top by growing his famous Tudor beard. Courtiers complimented the rotund ruler by wearing similar adornments, and Englishmen's faces began to bristle with whiskers so long and extravagant that the city fathers of London passed "An Acte Agaynst Bearded Men." Despite all legal restrictions, beards flourished and long hair came in again—possibly as the result of a new rash of complaints that barbers were employing diseased persons in their shops, where they "doo use and exercise barbery." More alarming was the charge that such "common artificers as Smythes, wevers, and women" were undertaking to perform "grete cures and thyngys of grete difficultie" under the sign of the barber's basin, and Henry issued a ruling that no barber henceforth be allowed to practice "letting of bludde, or any other thing belonging to surgery" except "drawing of teth."

With nothing to lose but a few molars, Elizabethan rakes and dandies repaired to the barbershop to smoke, sing and scribble sonnets. Lutes, viols and quill pens served to while away the long wait as the barber and his assistants painstakingly styled and stiffened beards in a variety of wondrous shapes. As the disapproving Puritan, Philip Stubbs, described it: "When you come to be trimmed, they will aske you whether you will be cut to look terrible to your enimie, or amiable to your freend, grim and sterne in countenance, or pleasant and demure" —the customers giving exact orders as to "how their mowchatowes must be preserved and laid out from one cheek to another, yea, almost from one eare to another, and turned up like two hornes towards the forehead."

Besides being curled, stiffened and clamped in a protective box at night, beards were often dyed. If an Elizabethan belle were moved to wonder "Doth he or doth he not tint his mowchatowes?" the chances were that he did—choosing the desired color from a spectrum so diverse that Shakespeare's Bottom names but a few in his *Midsummer Night's Dream* mention of "your straw colour beard, your orange-tawny beard, your purple-in-grain beard, or your French crown colour beard, your perfect yellow."

Of all hues, young bloods favored yellow and orange. Beards of these colors were worn as a pretty tribute to the Queen, whose own natural hair was reputed to be reddish blond—though few could say they had ever seen it, since Elizabeth usually wore a wig. The number of such regal head "attires" in the Queen's wardrobe has been estimated as 80 and valued at more than 8,000 guineas. Because of the high cost of human hair and the workmanship involved, few but the wealthiest women could afford to keep pace with the palace fashion. But the desire to own such a queenly "attire" eventually became so great that wig-snatching was a common crime and children were warned not to wander alone for fear of their being shorn by hair thieves.

During the reign of the first James, the hair of both

sexes remained in the care of barbers, hairdressers and wigmakers, though more and more men ventured to shave their own necks and cheeks with straight "cut-throat" razors. Mustaches and beards were gradually tapered into points, as though in preparation for dapper Charles I, who had his portrait painted wearing a trim triangular beard, to which posterity gave the name of the artist—Vandyke. The hair of Charles' courtly Cavaliers was long and sleek, and "spruse coxcombes" wore bow-tied "love-locks" and "heart-breakers" of hair that grew down to their chests. Against such unholy hairiness the Puritans aimed a barrage of testy treatises on the *Unloveliness of Love-locks* and *The Loathsomeness of Long Hair*—to which the laughing Cavaliers replied by dubbing their austerely clipped critics "Roundheads" and singing a ballad that inquired:

What creature's this, with his short hairs,
His little band, and huge long ears,
Which this new faith has founded?

In reality, the situation was far more complex than the song allows and Puritans had to struggle with their consciences every time they visited a barber. Too great a growth on head or chin marked a man as ungodly, but shaving clean and clipping too close gave the pious Protestants the unwanted appearance of Catholic priests. To solve this hairsplitting dilemma, some settled for the merest dab of beard beneath the lower lip, while others shaved clean and wore their locks fairly long. The latter dodge was chosen by Cromwell, who made his first appearance in Parliament with long hair, smooth chin, and two specks of blood on his white collar from having nicked his neck while shaving.

With the restoration of the Stuarts, all beards disappeared, mustaches faded from sight, and Wigsville became the fashion capital of Western Europe. While many English-speaking scholars credit Charles II as the bigwig most responsible for the triumph of the *outré* toupee, the monarch's fondness for false hairdos was something he picked up in France during exile at the court of Louis XIV. Louis, it seems, had such beautiful golden curls as a boy that courtiers took to wearing blond wigs in flattering imitation of the princely hairs and graces. Faced with baldness in his old age, Louis himself then wore enormous wigs, which were powdered white in keeping with his advanced years. Nobles and courtesans slavishly copied the royal rig, powdering their counterfeit curls with such convincing thoroughness that an ambassador from abroad was heard to exclaim in alarm at the sight of so many lovely young ladies with prematurely gray hair.

When Charles II and his elegant retinue arrived from France wearing similar way-out wigs, the English were only too eager to indulge their pent-up passion for anti-Puritan fun and fads and immediately set about to adopt the French *perruque*—roughly rendering the word as "peruke," "perwyke" and "periwig." Regardless of name, the prestige power of the powdered wig was soon recognized by English judges and lawyers—who still cling to the custom of wearing white wigs in court—and status-conscious Samuel Pepys scrupulously recorded the emotions and expense involved in maintaining a well-dressed head. "Comes Chapman the Perriwig maker," he wrote in 1663, "and he cut off my hair, which went a little to my heart to part with it; but it being over and my perriwig on I paid him £3 for it and awaye went he with my owne hair to make another of."

In addition to raising hair for his own wigs, the penny-wise Pepys found himself unwittingly engaged in the husbandry of some rather personal wildlife, as indicated in the following side glance into the intimate behavior of married couples during the rowdy and ribald Restoration. "So to my wife's chamber, and there supped, and got her cut off my hair and look my shirt, for I have itched mightily these 6 or 7 days, and when all comes to all she finds that I am lousy, having found in my head and body about twenty lice, little and great . . ." The peppy little pests all counted and exterminated, Pepys' hair problems were still not over, however. On a sleepy Sunday evening in 1668 the indiscreet diarist went to have his "head combed" by the willing young house-maid, Deb—an escapade "which occasioned the greatest sorrow to me that I ever knew in this world, for my wife, coming up suddenly, did find me embracing the girl."

Madame Pepys berated her wayward spouse until dawn of the following day, but it is unlikely that her anger was so great that she would have neglected to comb and brush her own "pair of perukes." Worn in wide puffs over the ears, these outrigger curls were, in contemporary description, "set on wyres to make them stand at a distance from the head; as the fardingales made their clothes stand out in Queen Elizabeth's reign." At one point in his diary Pepys foresaw the possibility of a decline in the peruke market following the Plague, "for nobody will dare to buy hair for fear of the infection, that it had been cut off the heads of people dead of the plague." But the English were more courageous than he supposed, and wigs continued to grow in popularity and size until, at the beginning of the eighteenth century, they covered the shoulders like a shawl and hung below the waist in back.

It was in this hair-hipped era that Alexander Pope penned his *Rape of the Lock*, a social satire that became a schoolroom classic despite the fact that it quite accurately detailed the psychosexual compulsions of an aging pre-Freudian hair fetishist. The object of his offbeat lust was the hair apparent of beautiful young Belinda, who, "to the destruction of mankind,"

Nourished two locks, which graceful hung behind
In equal curls . . .

So bewitching were these ringlets that they stimulated strange stirrings in the lopsided libido of the "adventurous baron," who finally achieved his erotic aim by snipping off the curls with a scissors. Shorn of the hair she prized most, Belinda angrily upbraided the baron and implied that he might have found her a willing enough victim to his odd amours if he had been content to seize "Hairs less in sight, or any hairs but these!"

By such tearful words of reproach, the half-tressed maiden betrayed her complete misunderstanding of the hair fetishist's quirks, since the deviation is confined almost exclusively to the hair of the female head. Women, on the other hand, are more likely to make a fetish of male baldness, for reasons which no psychologist has adequately explained. While the theory has been advanced that bald-headed men are apt to be sexually more vigorous by virtue of possessing an abundance of male hormones, the degeneration of the hair follicles preceding baldness has long been established as hereditary—the result of a man's inherited genes, having little or no relation to his prowess with acquired janes.

Intriguing in its own quaint way is the eighteenth-century theory of baldness which the bewigged Dr. Samuel Johnson quoted in his famous dictionary—"that the cause of baldness in men is dryness of the brain, and its shrinking from the skull." Absurd as the idea may sound, it must be acknowledged that if anything could have caused the cerebrum to dry up and shrink, it was the heat generated by period wigs. Even in winter an undercap was necessary to absorb the perspiration of the head, while the removal of the wig in a cold, damp room would often cause visible steam to rise from the scalp. To lessen the shock, turbans and nightcaps were worn indoors and fashionable men and women kept their wigs cool out of doors by carrying hats which they never wore, being specially designed to tuck under one arm.

What with the heat and humidity, male wigs began to diminish in size during the first half of the eighteenth century; but the number of styles increased. The basic style was the same pig-tailed peruke worn by colonial Americans, but there were various arrangements of bows and curls. To the modern eye, the differences are sometimes difficult to detect, but the sedan-chair and snuffbox set found it as easy to distinguish one from another as we do foreign cars. To name but a few models in the medium-to-luxury-price range, there were the Pigeon's Wing, the Royal Bird, the She-Dragon, the Cauliflower, the Crutch, the Rhinoceros, the Rose, the Ramillie, the Negligent, the Bag, the Wild Boar's Back, the Half-Natural and the Natty Scratch—each of which required a couple of pounds of flour a week to remain properly powdered.

Throughout Europe, the clean-shaven face had become a symbol of civilization and progress. Intent upon modernizing Russia, Peter the Great imposed a stiff tax on Slavic beards and roamed the palace, scissors in hand, clipping noblemen's whiskers in a one-man effort to overtake the West in the face race. In England daily "shaving of Face and Head" was recommended, and by 1759 the exaggerated claims of soap advertisers competing for the shaver's shillings were drawing critical fire from Dr. Johnson, who particularly objected to the copy used to promote "The True Royal Chymical Washball," an all-purpose soap guaranteed to "give an exquisite edge to the razor, and so comfort the brain and nerves as to prevent catching cold."

It remained for the beardless and affectedly brainless dandies of London's ultramodish Macaroni Club to push the wig to new heights when they adopted a high-piled peruke that came to a point on top, giving the head a Humpty-Dumpty appearance. Sweethearts and mistresses became enchanted with the new style and started a trend to high feminine hairdos that eventually towered two and three feet above the head. To gain the required altitude, a recipe in the *London Magazine* of 1768 calls for "False locks to supply deficiency of native hair, pomatum in profusion, greasy wool to bolster up the adopted locks, and gray powder to conceal dust." Since the time and expense of constructing such "pudding heads" was formidable, women slept on wooden neck rests and kept their well-caked coiffures untouched for three or more weeks—by which time the grease and flour would start smelling noticeably rancid. One hairdresser—a paragon of professional tact—is quoted as asking a particularly rich old customer "how long it was since her head had been opened and repaired; she answered not above nine weeks; to which he replied, that that was as long as a head could well go in summer; and that therefore it was proper to deliver it now, as it began to be a little *hasardé*."

At their most fanciful, the high-style "heads" were decorated with plumes, pearls, artificial fruits, model sailing ships, coaches, horses, and tiny figures arranged in storytelling scenes, like miniature Mardi Gras floats. In 1776 the British motif was occasionally political or military, as in the memorable "Bunker Hill" headdress which recreated the historic battle "with tents, fortifications, cannon and battalions" on the heights and a naval engagement over the forehead.

Prior to Bunker Hill and the Boston Tea Party, upper-class Americans wore wigs made to order in London, and Negro house slaves fabricated their own facsimilies from cotton, lamb's wool and goat hair. From the days of the Plymouth Puritans, natural hair was favored by farmers, artisans, merchants and sailors, and Harvard College anticipated the Ivy League cut with an early ruling aginst "Long haire, locks, foretops, curlings, crispings, partings or powdering of ye haire." American revolutionists were not inclined to make a political issue of the English powdered peruke, however, since many American royalists wore natural hair and many rebellious Whigs wore gentlemanly wigs—the name "Whig" having no hairy connotations at all, being derived from "whiggamores," a Scotch word for wagon drivers, who once "marched on Edinburgh to oppose the king."

It was Rousseau and the class-conscious French Revolutionists who first flipped the wigs of the aristocrats. "The poor must go without bread because we must have powder for our hair," the philosopher wrote in protest against the annual loss of tons of flour used in whitening French perukes; and with the outbreak of mob violence both wigs and heads were lopped off by the guillotine. Tyranny was fought with tousled hair, and bravos of the barricades had their heads roughly cropped in the rebellious "Brutus" style. Liberal sympathizers in Europe and America discarded wigs and wore their hair clipped and mussed as a matter of democratic principle. English women, conscious of the rabble-rousing potentialities of high hairdos, brought their "heads" down from the chandeliers and combed their long tresses into soft, romantic streams. As an aftermath of crop failures and bread riots, Prime Minister Pitt then delivered the coup de grace to the English wig by instituting a guinea tax on hair powder, which earned conspicuous consumers the scornful name of "guinea pigs."

In less than a decade, the once-universal wig disappeared. For the first time in history, women of France wore their hair in short curls and donned flesh-colored underpants to conceal their maidenhair from public view as they strolled the rues and boulevards in the sheer muslin gowns David, the artist, designed and immortalized in oils. Equally permanent were the grease spots Englishmen were beginning to leave on the backs of upholstered chairs—spots resulting from the lavish use of hair lotions, such as Rowland's Macassar Oil. To combat the greasy menace, upholstery was pinned with protective lace doilies, which came to be known as "antimacassars."

No mere doily, however, could withstand the penetrating power of Rowland's biggest competitor—bear grease—the commercial handling of which is tellingly revealed in a snatch of period advertising copy: "H. LITTLE, Perfumer, No. 1 Portugal Street, Lincoln's Inn Fields, acquaints the Public that he has killed a remarkable fine RUSSIAN BEAR, the fat of which is matured by time to a proper state. He begs leave to solicit their attention to this Animal, which, for its fatness and size, is a real curiosity. He is now selling the fat, cut from the Animal, in boxes at 2s. 6d. and 5s. each, or rendered down into pots, from One Shilling . . ."

In the as-yet-untamed United States, dead bears were less of a novelty, and young Yankees used the grizzly grease to dress their hair in the free-flowing style made popular by the dashing Lord Byron. Long sideburns began to develop into "muttonchop" cheek whiskers that gradually crept down under the chin to form a fringe beard, and young bucks on both sides of the Atlantic cultivated the long-lost mustache with the enthusiasm of rare-orchid fanciers. "The mustaches are glorious, glorious," young Charles Dickens wrote to a fellow devotee in 1844. "I have cut them shorter and trimmed them a little at the ends to improve their shape. They are charming, charming. Without them life would be a blank."

Happily for the creator of Fezziwig and Chuzzlewit, life during the reign of the bunned and braided Victoria was one merry round of mustaches and beards. All the square-cut, round-cut, pointed, forked and fan-tailed prodigies of the past were revived, and long, drooping "Dundrearies" and "Piccadilly Weepers" swept the starched shirt fronts and obscured the somber cravats. By 1860, the appeal of the beard was such that a committee of New York Republicans urged their clean-shaven presidential candidate, A. Lincoln, to "cultivate whiskers and wear standing collars" as a sure-fire means of capturing the popular vote. "All the ladies like whiskers and they would tease their husbands to vote for you," a little girl named Grace Bedell wrote in a letter recommending the same sort of political growth. Lincoln wisely accepted the advice, and a bearded "Father Abraham" became the central figure in the War Between the States.

Granted the number of beardless youths who fought in blue and gray, the Civil War must go on record as the hairiest in American history, the combined foliage of any ten generals being sufficient to stuff a horsehair sofa—the cheek whiskers of one general, Ambrose Everett Burnside, achieving a kind of immortality in a now-familiar switch on the Union leader's last name: "sideburn."

In the postwar years, veterans wearing tumbleweed whiskers and tobacco-stained mustaches continued to settle the wild and woolly West, where Indian scalpers had their own notions of how a white man should be trimmed. According to the Reverend E. Cobham Brewer, the Cheyennes "remove from the part just over the left ear a piece of skin not larger than a silver dollar. The Arrapahoes take a similar piece from the region of the right ear," while the Utes "take the entire scalp from ear to ear, and from the forehead to the nape of the neck."

Meanwhile, back at the barbershop, city slickers and Main Street dudes were abandoning "old fogy" beards for heavy waxed mustaches that curled up at the ends like the steering gear on one of the newfangled bicycles. "That mustache looks like a handle bar," some wisecracker exclaimed, and the joke was carried to barbershops all over the country by backslapping traveling men, who parted their hair in the middle and brushed both sides at once with a pair of military brushes. Often the only roots a traveling salesman had was a shaving mug with his name on it standing in the mug rack of some barbershop. The local customer kept his mug there, too, its presence entitling him to all the social privileges of the place—such as singing in an impromptu quartet, ogling the big-hipped beauties in *The Police*

Gazette, and gazing out the window in hopes of catching a glimpse of ankle at the corner horsecar stop.

In the eighties and nineties the clublike atmosphere was elevated to gaslit splendor in the big-city "tonsorial parlor," a luxurious masculine refuge replete with white marble, black leather upholstery, mahogany cabinetwork and mirrored walls. In the sparkle of its brass spittoons, cut-glass decanters and tall bottles of red, green and yellow tonic, the large metropolitan barbershop rivaled the glittering decor of a plush saloon or carriage-trade sporting house. If in a sociable mood, a man was assured of conversation that ranged from politics and stocks and bonds to prize fights, race horses and women. To the soothing slipslap rhythm of the leather razor strop, the thoughtful could retreat behind a newspaper selected from a convenient rack where each daily was hung in a split bamboo clip. Amidst a comforting medley of floral scents, the gleaming hot-towel machine puffed steamy promises of relaxation to the weary, who found in the barber's reclining chair all the restful benefits of modern "heart-saver" seating. Here was no quick clip-and-tip. The leisurely therapy of shampoo, shave, hot towel and scalp massage sent a man forth into the world with his psyche refreshed and his face aglow with the tingle of bay rum.

As America twenty-three-skiddooed into the twentieth century, Grandpa was still combing his whiskers and father was still drinking his morning coffee from a mustache cup—a convenient piece of china with a built-in shield across the top to keep his handle bars out of the hot java. His up-to-the-minute collegiate son laughingly called the "old man's" mustache a "soup strainer" or "cookie duster," while father scowled at the thin line of growth on the young whippersnapper's upper lip and muttered something about a "misplaced eyebrow."

The outbreak of the war in Europe in 1914 found a bearded king in England, a mustached Premier in France, a clean-shaven Chief Executive in the White House, and a German Kaiser with—as the Elizabethan Puritan Philip Stubbs once put it—mustaches "turned up like two hornes towards the forehead" to make himself "look terrible" to his enemies. When American forces entered the conflict under mustached General Pershing, Army barbers worked overtime mass-producing close-cropped "coolie haircuts" with mechanical hand clippers and King C. Gillette's ingenious safety razors were issued to recruits. Originally marketed in 1903 at five dollars, the handy little shavers were then priced at a dime—though country boys using the gadget for the first time declared it couldn't shave worth a cent. Hundreds were thrown away before it was discovered that the strawfoots were putting the blades in their razors without removing the wax-paper wrapping.

In the peace that followed, barbers began to rely heavily on electric clippers. With the aid of these buzzing marvels, neck hair was trimmed so high and close that customers felt cheated unless the rearview mirror reflected a clean display of talcumed skull bone behind each ear. "See you got a haircut," one sport would remark to another. "No, I didn't," the postwar wag would reply. "Had my ears lowered instead!" Even more uproarious was the laughter which greeted the suggestion that a man in need of a haircut should "buy a violin." Long hair was strictly for artists and musicians, while beards were for bolsheviks, bohemians and bums.

Allowing for variations in tonsorial artistry, haircuts of the twenties were remarkably standardized. Shieks and sugar daddies were clipped and trimmed in pretty much the same "regular" style as bookkeepers and bootleggers, and the vast majority of American males shaved at home. Balancing the barbers' loss was the fact that increasing numbers of women were visiting barbershops to have their hair shingled and bobbed. Once considered the hallmark of a mannish radical, the short shingle was now being worn by daring young flappers and gin-slinging jazz babies, who flattened their bosoms and donned straight-cut sacks in the mistaken belief that sexual emancipation demanded that they look and act like gay young boys. In 1922 the *American Hairdresser*, trade organ of the beauty-shop interests, confidently predicted that the bobbed-hair craze would "not last through the summer." But the convenience of short hair proved so attractive that most women in the Western world had their hair bobbed by 1930, touching off a wave of business failures among hairdressers and manufacturers of hairpins, nets and curling irons. Only with the onset of the Depression in the thirties did the trade begin to recover. Women, faced with the loss of gilt-edged securities and diamond jewelry, were forced to fall back on their physical assets. Clothes were designed to emphasize the womanly wealth of the figure, and hair gradually fell to shoulder length in the sexy Hollywood styles of Ann Sheridan, Rita Hayworth and Lana Turner.

During the same money-shy decade, most men got a haircut only when they needed it and shook their heads firmly to the barber's hopeful litany of extras: "Shave? Shampoo? A little tonic?" In 1932 the price of a haircut was seldom more than thirty-five cents and a nickel tip was considered sufficient. If a customer didn't mind killing an hour reading back issues of *Ballyhoo*, he could "wait for the boss" and eliminate the need for a tip. The boss was presumed to be so rich that he didn't need the nickel.

Determined to keep up a presentable appearance, the more heroic among the unemployed subjected themselves to the uncertain skills of barber-college students, who charged a dime for a haircut and five cents for a shaky shave. At home, penny-wise shavers whisked away the bristles with single- and double-edged safety razors and experimented with patented blade sharpeners whose thrifty appeal paralleled that of the roll-your-own cigarette machine. While professional barbers continued to suffer from the slump, the market for home shaving products boomed and advertisers poured millions into the promotion of brushless shaving creams. On radio Singin' Sam, the Barbasol Man, crooned the new no-brush theme in a lusty baritone. On the highways motorists developed a quoting acquaintance with groups of signboards strung along the side of the road, each displaying one line of a brushless-cream jingle: "To get away . . . From hairy apes . . . Ladies jump . . . From fire escapes. . . . Burma Shave."

As America pulled uphill into the forties the economy recovered to the point where merchandisers began to find a market for prestige-type razors, such as a premium-priced English job with a permanent sword-steel blade and a lifetime honing strop built into the case. The first Schick Injector razor made a bid for attention with the "push-pull-click-click" of its automatic blade changer, and the price of a haircut climbed to fifty cents. Tips went up to a dime, but millions of able-bodied Americans were getting G.I. haircuts at government expense. Whether given in a barber's chair at a Stateside base or while seated on an oilcan on Okinawa, the standard service clip was short and speedy. But despite the jokes and griping about the G.I. cut, many discharged veterans continued to wear it in the postwar years, when it became known as the crew cut—a cognomen that suggested college athletics under the G.I. Bill of Rights. In its original form, the crew cut featured closely clipped sides and an inch of hair on top. If the top hair were longer, it was a feather crew. Cut straight across the head in a short, stiff brush, it was a flat top. Rounded to the shape of the skull, it was a butch. At the opposite extreme were the long hairstyles of some younger-generation males, whose carefully combed locks swirled to a crest in back like a duck's tail feathers—hence the "D.A." or Duck's Ass.

With industry retooling for peacetime production, the Army's aerosol bug bomb was adapted to civilian use and brushless creams were canned under pressure to eject a spurt of aerated foam at the touch of a finger. But in the late forties and early fifties many men were switching from safety razors to electric shavers amidst a cross fire of advertising claims. One shaver boasted "the largest shaving head of them all," designed to get at the "Hidden Beard!" Another prided itself on the thinness and flexibility of its shaving surface and rather churlishly retorted, "Other shavers have thick rigid heads!" Alert to his consumer responsibilities, the average American male compared the differences between each year's improved models, trading in the old and trial-testing the new with the same kind of tire-kicking concentration he brought to the purchase of a new car.

Sensing an undertone of status yearning in the electric-shaver phenomenon, one safety-razor firm successfully launched a gold-plated model in 1953. But the safety razor's strongest appeal was, and is, its low cost and upkeep—a point which was underscored by the widespread acceptance of the new "twenty-shave" stainless-steel blades in 1963. In preparation for the continued coexistence of two shaving methods, purveyors of lotions and talcs shrewdly angled their lines to lure both the electric-shaver and safety-razor customers and in 1961 were recommending "pre-shave" lotions to "prop up" the beard for a wet electric shave.

During the battle of blades and beard mowers, the crew cut evolved into the conservative "Ivy League" and was perfectly in keeping with the trend to natural shoulders and narrow lapels. Introduced into the image-conscious precincts of advertising and television, the unassuming tonsure was modestly parted and brushed flat to give even the gray-haired an appearance of boyish sincerity. Now called the "Madison Avenue," it could be seen bobbing affably in the charcoal-gray crowd as the curates of communications and the high priests of persuasion hastened to their noonday devotions. Mingled in the midtown throng one also sees, of late, the "Caesar" —a modified "Madison Avenue" brushed forward on the head in the manner of the bald Roman Julius.

During the early sixties it seemed that the younger man's preference was for a short haircut, while many mature types were going halfway with a semi-crew, known as the "Dutch," the "Detroit" or the "California." More recently, however, the nation's better barbershops have reported a trend to longer hair in the "Continental" or "British" style, typified by Rex Harrison and Sir Harold Macmillan; and the brief but strongly vital New Frontier brought an increasing number of requests for haircuts "like President Kennedy's."

Since no one had ever been known to request a trim like Dwight D. Eisenhower's or Harry S. Truman's, interest in the Kennedy cut could hardly be attributed to politics. It was, in fact, a result of the late President's personal sense of style—a quality possessed to an even greater degree by his attractive young First Lady. Months before the President's nomination, Jacqueline Kennedy's bouffant coiffure was causing more comment, pro and con, than any other woman's hairstyle in recent history. In addition to inspiring a postelection boom in "Jackie" hairdos, Mrs. Kennedy delighted professional hairdressers the world over by having her hair done twice a day during her triumphant visit to Paris. For a banquet at the Elysée Palace her hair was arranged in the mode of a Renaissance "Madonna." For a reception at Versailles Alexandre of Paris "dressed her cheeks" with poufs of hair in the seventeenth-century style of one of Louis XIV's mistresses. The press could not have been more atwitter if she had shown up in Charlemagne's beard.

Newsworthy, too, was the invitation President Kennedy's New York barber, Louis Bocchetto, received to the Inaugural Ball. Besieged by customers' requests to duplicate the Kennedy haircut, Mr. Bocchetto loyally refused. "Not all men look like Mr. Kennedy, or have hair like Mr. Kennedy's," he was quoted as saying, "and on the majority of men it would look foolish."

In so commenting, Mr. Bocchetto revealed himself to be a true "hair stylist," dedicated to creating custom haircuts that suit the individual. Though his rates were reported to be moderate by Manhattan standards, this sort of personalized service is beginning to command prices that promise to rival the fees charged for a psychoanalytic hour. At present, customers at one hoity-toity tonsorial salon are being clipped at the rate of $20 a haircut. Another charges $4 for a styling and $2.50 for a cut. The basic "works," which includes shampoo, shave and manicure, totals $12, sans tip—a price that gives new significance to the traditional bleeding basin atop the blood-red pole.

The mere ability to pay does not make one eligible for a haircut at one of New York's top-status shops, however. There service is available only to a select group of privileged regulars. The presence of one's name in the appointment book is considered tantamount to membership in the French Academy of Immortals, and the well-heeled pledgee is required to take his place on a waiting list pending the eventual death of ten elder clients. To survive the long wait with a modicum of prestige, applicants often resort to the office haircut, given at one's desk—a tycoon-type ritual initiated by the Emperor Augustus, who would call in two or three barbers to give him a shave and trim while he dictated memos in Latin.

To justify higher prices, barbers attending the 1960 National Barber Show were told that the haircut "must be perfect. . . . We don't want to have to look down when we tell the customer $4.50." In order to maintain a cool, steady gaze at the moment of truth, some barbers have been reducing their patrons to a state of humble reverence by giving haircuts with a straight-edge razor —a technique more ancient than Rome, with a primitive kinship to Maori obsidian-knife ceremonies. While the customer need not eat a sacrificial victim or perform incantations against thunder and lightning, he must yet be on his guard against the modern barber's mumbo jumbo of bewitching extras. "Don't forget eyebrow coloring," one razor-wielding stylist told his fellow clip-artists at the show. "That's the fastest buck you ever made. A man's eyebrows get bleached by the sun; it makes his face look weak. I get $1.50 for that, $2.50 for a mustache job."

At the moment, there seems to be no immediate danger of a return to "orange-tawny" mowchatowes or "purple-in-grain" eyebrows, but the recent resurgence of the beard has caused many urban barbers to brush up on the Elizabethan art of pogonotomy, or beard trimming. In the London of the present-day Elizabeth, one posh practitioner has been specializing in a Byronesque male permanent called the "Tiara-Boom D.A.," while another emulates the Egyptians with custom-designed false beards for evening wear. Add to these the "Caesar," the Augustan office haircut and the increasing demand for toupees and it would appear that the future of shaves and haircuts is rooted firmly in the past.

As this brief history is being trimmed and manicured for the press, American teen types mimic the mop-top modes of the Beatles with overgrown "Soup-bowl" styles that are but the kooky counterpart of those worn by Kings Henry II through V. As a harbinger of cutless cuts to come, the New York *Times* appears with a neatly clipped headline: "British 'His and Her' Hairdos Blur 'Him-Her' Line." "Teen-age couples in London have a new way of pledging their affections—by wearing their hair alike," Gloria Emerson cables in a special *Times* report. "The most commonly seen hairdo, acidly described as 'British togetherness,' is marked by a thick Beatle fringe over the forehead, long sideburns that could be spitcurls, and a shaggy shingle effect in the back. More startling are the shoulder-length lionlike hairdos worn by other young men and their girl friends. . . ."

With both Mods and Rockers affecting he-lion-she-lion manes, sexual confusion is such that young men are frequently mistaken for girls, Miss Emerson reports, while older Britons "smile wanly and blame the influence of popular singers, such as the Beatles (the best groomed), the Rolling Stones, the Pretty Things, the Animals, the Kinks, the Dave Clark Five and the Daisies." Of all such non-barbershop singers, the Pretty Things have provoked the most hostility among parents and teachers. Male Pretty-Thing fans who show up for class "wearing long hair in the quasi-Stuart fashion," are often threatened with suspension, given hairnets, or "forced to tie their hair back with ribbons"—a practice which has led some observers to predict a return of seventeenth-century "love locks" and the beribboned eighteenth-century male pigtail.

At a time when wigs are in big with the fair sex and feminine hairstyles approach the heights of the "pudding-head" coiffures of old, the possibility of a twentieth-century revival of a pigtailed, powdered and beribboned "Natty Scratch" for American men may not be as remote as we would like to believe, and the alert citizen can hardly be blamed for looking up with a nervous start when the smiling gent in the starched white coat calls out a cheery, "Next?"

III

BATHING

Bathing

More ancient than the custom of shaving and cutting hair is the habit of bathing—the human practice of which began with Early Man, and is presumed to have developed from the experience of getting wet. Though it probably evolved only after a long period of scratching and laughing, it preceded the use of soap by thousands of years and has figured prominently in the histories of religion, sex, medicine and Madison Avenue.

Since time immemorial people have bathed in the sacred waters of the Nile and the Ganges. According to Herodotus, the priests of ancient Egypt bathed religiously "twice every day, and twice every night." Bathsheba was taking a bath when she first attracted the adulterous attentions of King David, who saw her from the roof of his house and found her "very beautiful to look upon." *Leviticus* demands that the man and woman who "shall lie with seed of copulation . . . shall both bathe themselves in water"; and when the beauteous Esther sought to win the favor of King Ahasuerus she was bathed and scented for a whole year: "to wit, six months with oil of myrrh, and six months with sweet odors, and with other things for the purifying of the women."

Homer has it that the gods and goddesses of ancient Greece took baths as a prelude to seduction. When Hera saw Zeus seated upon Mt. Ida, she began to scheme how to "entice him to lie by her side in love, so that quiet and balmy sleep might drown his eyes and mind.

"So she went to her chamber . . . She closed the doors, and first she washed every speck and stain from her lovely body with a bath of ambrosia. She annointed her body with oil, ambrosial, soft, scented with perfumes . . ."

While it's hardly surprising that the ox-eyed goddess should have laved her body in ambrosia, it is somewhat remarkable that she took her bath in private, without the assistance of handmaidens. The mortal Odysseus, for example, was constantly having his back scrubbed by obliging females. When he set sail from Calypso's isle, the fair-haired nymph saw him off only "after she had bathed him and clothed him in garments scented with juniper." The sportive maidens who attended Nausicaä could hardly be restrained from helping him bathe alfresco in a river, and at the palace of Alcinoüs "the women bathed him and rubbed him with oil."

But such merry arrangements were makeshift in comparison to the organized sweating and splashing that took place in the classical Greek gymnasium. Here the naked Hellenes wrestled and romped in glistening coats of olive oil, which were later sweated away in steam rooms. From thence they nipped into a cold bath, donned fresh linen, and spent the afternoon at philosophic discourses in an adjoining lecture hall.

It was on this high-minded model that the Romans built their first public baths, which soon expanded into vast pleasure domes where the accent was on hot water, steaming vapor and scented sensuality. Philosophy and athletics were washed down the magnificently engineered drains, and the discourses of the bath were no longer Platonic. Although the men were ostensibly separated from the women, slaves of the opposite sex were commonly employed as bath attendants, and Montaigne reports that it was the custom for ladies "to receive men in the vapor baths" for steamy assignations.

"Who was ever worse than Nero? What could be better than Nero's baths?" the poet Martial asked—for it was the fat-necked emperor with the legendary fiddle who gave Rome its first taste of bathing on the grand scale when he constructed a handsome bath on the Palatine Hill in the hope of diverting public attention from his pyromania, parricide and other assorted pranks. In his own Golden House, where dinner guests were sprayed with fragrances from concealed sprinklers, the malodorous tyrant kept both sea water and sulphur water on tap in the opulent baths. Poppaea, his sometime wife, preferred to bathe in asses' milk, however, and cultivated the art of erotic soaking to the point where she could recommend bathing in a solution of benzoin and dusting with powdered starch to the young lady who wished to "pass as a virgin."

Harking back to the virtuous simplicity of the old days, when Romans "bathed their whole bodies on market days only"—and then in plain stone tubs—Seneca asked, "Who at this time would submit to bathe thus?" The dour dramatist scorned the grandeur of the baths, with their statuary, precious marble and silver pipes. "Since dainty baths have been invented, we are become more nasty," he charged. "Horace, when describing a man infamous for his dissipation, what does he charge him with? With smelling of perfumed balls—*Pastillos Rufillus olet!*"

With this allusion to early cakes of scented soap, Seneca shortly departed this life. Ordered by Nero to kill himself, he botched his suicide and ironically expired in the suffocating heat of the furnace room of his own private bath. Following the equally ignoble death of Nero, the pitch of Roman luxury mounted, as each succeeding emperor sought to ensure his popularity by providing bigger and more sumptuous public baths. The Baths of Caracalla were a mile in circumference and contained theaters, temples and festival halls. The massive main building was regarded as a paragon of public architecture as late as the nineteenth century, when it was used as the model for the construction of New York's Pennsylvania Station. Diocletian's Baths, completed in 302

A.D., were more magnificent still and could accommodate 32,000 bathers in pools heated to varying degrees of temperature.

But the decline of Rome was already under way, and with the collapse of the Western Empire the unsupervised baths became sinkholes of crime and depravity. Christians, who had labored in slave battalions to build the baths, denounced them as pagan works. Cleanliness was held akin to devilishness, the buildings fell into disrepair and were abandoned, and the odor of sanctity became indistinguishable from B.O.

The reaction of the Eastern Christians in Constantinople was more moderate, and the practice of bathing was preserved largely through the influence of the Greeks, whose forefathers had introduced the classical steam-and-water treatment into Africa and Asia. The slow spread of the art among Arabic nations is typified by the story of Abooseer, an itinerant bath-keeper, as related in *The Thousand and One Nights:* "So when Abooseer knew that there was not a Bath in the city . . . he repaired to the council of the King, and went in to him, and having kissed the ground before him and prayed for him, said to him, 'I am a man of a strange country, and my trade is that of a Bath-keeper, and I entered thy city, and desired to repair to the Bath, but saw not in it even one Bath; and how is it that a city of this beautiful description is without a Bath, which is one of the best delights of the world?' So the King said to him, 'What is the Bath?' "

Starting, so to speak, from scratch, Abooseer described its wonders, and the King ordered such a building to be constructed. When it was finished, "Abooseer invited the King to the Bath. So he mounted, with the great men of his empire, and they went thither. He pulled off his clothes and entered the inner department; and Abooseer entered and rubbed the King with the bag, removing from his person the impure particles like twists of thread, and showing them to him, whereat the King rejoiced . . . After Abooseer had washed his skin, he mixed for him some rose water with the water of the tank; and the King descended into the tank and came forth, and his skin was softened, and he experienced a liveliness which in his life he had never known before. Then after that Abooseer seated him upon the raised floor, and the Mamelukes proceeded to perform on him the operation of gently rubbing and pressing him, while the perfuming vessels diffused the odor of aloewood. And the King said, 'O master! is this the Bath?' Abooseer answered 'Yes.' And the King said to him, 'By my head, my city hath not become a city, save by this Bath!' "

It was the enthusiasm of just such satisfied customers that led to the construction of hundreds of baths throughout the Middle East at a time when their popularity was supposedly on the wane in Europe. There are evidences, however, that some Roman baths, built in northern outposts for the military, continued to operate for the benefit of local civilians, and mixed bathing parties enabled Germanic friends and neighbors to see each other socially throughout the Middle Ages. According to one account, "Everybody undressed at home and went to the baths practically naked. . . . The men went into the baths wearing a suspensory; on their entering, an attendant handed them a bundle of rods, intended for massage; the women's bathing costume consisted of a diminutive apron which usually slipped off the hips. The bathers had to be administered to by the opposite sex."

With "robust waiters" and "trim waitresses" in attendance, and the customers' complete freedom to mingle, the erotic atmosphere of the medieval German baths exceeded that of the Romans'. In time they became little more than public brothels and houses of assignation, where the emphasis was less on hygiene than it was on sexual high jinks of the most crude and obvious sort. As one contemporary couplet put it:

Nothing better than a bath for the woman sterile,
For with the water goes company virile.

The author was Giovanni Francesco Poggio Bracciolini, who visited the communal baths at Baden in the late Middle Ages. But St. Boniface is known to have issued a prohibition against mixed nude bathing as early as the year 745, and pictorial art of the period offers ample evidence that the feudal bath was a centuries-long bash. Aprons and suspensories were discarded in favor of birthday suits, and fashionable ladies were wont to express their feminine chic in ornate headdresses and hats. Gentlemen, too, were given to wearing hats in the tub and are to be seen in all their neck-up propriety assisting their dames in the offices of the bath with much amorous feeling. Beds were provided in curtained alcoves, musicians were employed to serenade the bathers, and one illuminating old manuscript illustration shows a group of gay Gothic couples disporting themselves at a buffet supper served from a table set up in the large, communal tub.

The greatest impetus to social bathing in England and France occurred during the Crusades, when knights, squires and camp-following servant wenches became acquainted with the rose-scented delights of the Islamic bath. Indeed, the present-day Order of the Bath is supposed to have originated with the traditional top-to-toe tubbing that knights received at the hands of young virgins. Parsifal, Tristram, Guy of Warwick and other chivalrous chaps all enjoyed such maidenly ministrations, and a contemporary illustration depicts one nonchalant knight relaxing in his tub while a bevy of adoring young females showers him with rose petals.

Prior to the Crusades, the English attitude toward water was one of extreme caution. Though water was acknowledged to be useful in putting out fires, few chose to drink it unless it had been "cleansed and pourged by boylynge," for it was believed to be "infect with frogges and other wormes that brede." Pure springs and "holy welles" were used mainly for medicinal purposes and were under the protection of monks and friars, while the average Englishman drank ale and scrupulously avoided dampness.

Wine, Women, Baths, by art or Nature warm,
Used or abused do men much good or harm.

Such was the prudent message contained in a lively Latin tract on hygiene which William the Conqueror's son, Robert, received from the learned doctors of Salerno in 1096. But once the fad for bathing took hold, the immoderate and simultaneous pursuit of all three warm pleasures soon earned the public baths a reputation for being *seminaria venenata*, or seminaries of sex and sensuality. It was many a young wife's tale that she had become pregnant merely from bathing in water that had previously been used by a man, and the superstition arose that male bath water was dangerously potent with "frogges and other wormes" of fertility. Sir Thomas Browne found such stories "common in every mouth" in the twelfth century and sought to scotch them by declaring that it was impossible to thus "fornicate at a distance, and much offendeth the rules of Physick."

As in Germany and France, the English baths, or "stews," became resorts for lower-class lust and prostitution. The name "stewhouse" served to designate both public baths and brothels, just as the Italians used *bagnio* for either a bathhouse or a bordello. Wealthier people and nobles were inclined to be more exclusive and usually bathed at home. But illicit passions thrived on limited privacy, and tubbing as a twosome was a popular get-acquainted gambit with upper-class couples. If found *flagrante delicto*, errant lovers could logically plead that they were only trying to save water—no small consideration at a time when it had to be purchased by the bucketful from professional water-bearers or hauled by hand from a town pump (which convenience, incidentally, appears in early records as a *pompe*, *pymp*, *pimp* or *plump*).

Toward the end of the fifteenth century the old association between wantonness and water began to dissolve.

With repeated ravages of plagues and two major outbreaks of the "sweating sickness," public baths were closed as breeding places of infection and the habit of personal cleanliness was all but forgotten. As Max von Boehn, the German student of modes and manners, described it: "Ladies and gentlemen of the sixteenth century arrayed themselves in the most costly fabrics; they were stiff with velvets, silks and gold brocades; they were positively plastered with pearls and precious stones; and—they stank like the plague!"

Throughout the century pestilence continued to sweep Europe, but few suspected that the cause might be found in the lack of civic sanitation. In the cities, stables and open-pit privies were almost as numerous as houses and shops and the streets were narrow and strewn with filth. The habit of emptying chamber pots out of upper-story windows into the gutter made a city stroll so hazardous that gentlemen gallantly took the side nearest the curb when walking with their ladies—a position they have assumed ever since, without quite knowing why.

Modern readers who wonder at the fuss made over Sir Walter Raleigh's throwing his cloak across a puddle for Good Queen Bess need only acquaint themselves with the pollution of Elizabethan puddles to realize the magnificence of the gesture. But of all the heroes, wits and courtiers who surrounded the Virgin Queen, only one man responded to the situation with true genius. His name was Sir John Harington, and he invented the single most important piece of plumbing in the modern bathroom: the flush toilet.

To include this now-familiar facility as part of the bath is a peculiarly American idea, historically resisted by most of the world's peoples. Even today, travelers in Europe will often find the toilet or "W.C." enshrined in its own little closet, quite apart from the tub. Sometimes it is even outside the house—a location fraught with inconvenience and redolent of historical and religious tradition.

The ancient Hindus, for example, were enjoined to retire to the distance of a bowshot from the house with a brass vessel. Members of the Hebraic Essene sect were provided with small paddles with which to dig suitable holes in out-of-the-way places. The Egyptians were a privy people, and the rhymed advice of Hesiod offers partial insight into the outdoor habits of the Greeks:

Stand not upright before the eye of day;
And scatter not your water as you go,
Nor let it, when you're naked, from you flow:
In either case 'tis an unseemly sight:
The gods observe alike by day and night:
The man whom we devout and wise may call
Sits in that act, or streams against a wall.

When bathing was at its height in Rome, luxurious latrines with marble seats were built directly over the sewers that sluiced down from the hills and tubs were placed at street corners to serve as urinals. Trimalchio, the rich man's rich man, whom Petronius profiled in the *Satyricon*, was attended by a eunuch who followed him about with a silver chamber pot. While "playing at ball with a company of boys," the decadent tycoon "snapp'd his fingers, at which sign the eunuch held the chamber pot to him as he was playing; then calling for water, he dipped the tips of his fingers in it, and dry'd them on the boy's head."

In the absence of fleet-footed eunuchs and short boys with bushy hair, the feudal lord repaired to a rude wooden privy along with his vassals. Affluent barons had indoor facilities tucked away in castle closets with narrow window slits, which some Victorian romancers believed to be crossbow vents. Others mistook the tiny closets for cloakrooms or small chapels intended for princely meditation. In any case, the fitting consisted of a wooden seat placed over an open shaft, which ran down the outside wall and emptied into the moat. If the *Nuremberg Chronicle* is to be believed, it was through one such shaft that a certain proud nobleman was attacked by enemy archers. The castle, one need hardly add, was instantly surrendered.

The public privies, or "jakes," of medieval cities were plain wooden-plank affairs built over deep pits—and risky rest rooms they were. At times the board seats would rot out and citizens would fall through. Since rolls of tissue were unheard of, each crude comfort station was supplied with a curved stick for the use of all and sundry. In the darkness of night it was often impossible to decide which end of the tool to grab, and unlucky guessers were heard to complain of getting "the moocky end of the stick."

Indoors, finer folk used chamber pots placed in ornamental boxes with comfortably padded seats. These were known as "close stools," and Thomas Dekker gave satiric advice to Elizabethan status seekers on their correct social use: "You may rise at dinner-time to aske for a close-stoole, protesting to all the gentlemen that it costs you a hundred pounds a yeare in physicke, besides the Annual pension which your wife allowes her Doctor: and (if you please) you may (as your great French Lord doth) invite some speciall friend of yours, from the table, to hold discourse with you as you sit in that withdrawing-chamber: from whence being returned againe to the board, you shall sharpen the wits of all the eating Gallants about you, and doe them great pleasure to aske what Pamphlets or poems a man might think fittest to wipe his taile with . . ."

In the year 1596 someone was almost certain to propose a new work by Sir John Harington, the aforementioned Father of the Flush Toilet, for it was thought a scurrilous bit of whimsey. The work was called *The Metamorphosis of Ajax* (or "a jakes"), and in its pages the aptly named Sir John gave the world complete details for the construction of a simple water closet and cesspool—or, in his own words, "Plan Plots of a Privy in Perfection." Genius that he was, Sir John was yet a man before his time. Though his godmother, the Queen, had a working model built in Richmond Palace, where a copy of operating instructions hung hopefully from a peg, the ingenious device served mainly as a witty whatnot to amuse palace visitors and was widely ridiculed.

This, then, was sanitation's darkest hour. But some thinking men were beginning to advocate at least a modicum of bodily cleanliness. "I look upon bathing as generally salubrious," Montaigne confessed, "and believe that we suffer in health to no small degree for having left off the custom." The majority, who feared moisture and favored crud, persisted, however, despite the fact that many advanced medical practitioners prescribed hot mineral baths for a variety of human ills, including "Preternatural Thirst, All Sorts of Worms" and "the Longing of Maids to eat Chalk, Coals and the Like."

In France, where physicians believed that male glands were prone to become congested with stones and sediment, Montaigne found some experts who claimed, "It is a good thing to have frequent intercourse with women, for that opens the passages and carries away the gravel and sand," while others declared it "very bad, because it inflames, wearies and weakens the kidneys." Similarly others said: "It is a good thing to take hot baths, since that relaxes the places where the sand and stone settle; it is also a bad thing, because the application of external heat assists the kidneys in baking, hardening and petrifying the matter there stored up."

While French kings and courtesans possessed baths of considerable splendor, bathing was extremely occasional and wariness of water continued into the eighteenth century, when the arts of powdering and perfuming reached their apogee. The Marquise de Pompadour spent an estimated 1,000,000 pounds a year on fragrances, and it was rumored that Du Barry secreted scented pads about her person in order to seduce Louis XV. Most people were quite content with their own natural aroma, however. When an outspoken lady friend told Samuel Johnson that he "smelled," the gamy and garrulous doctor had no quarrel with the intent of her statement but expressed great concern over her misuse of verbs. "You *smell*," he corrected; "I *stink*."

In the first half of the eighteenth century the pro-water wing of the medical profession began to propagandize in earnest. Upper-class faddists made it fashionable to wash the hands, face and neck every day, and persons of means resorted to Tunbridge Wells, Epsom and Bath to take "the cure."

Of all English watering places, Bath was the richest in tradition. Supposedly founded by King Lear's father, Bladud, who had been cured of leprosy by bathing with his pigs in the hot, bubbling mud of the springs, the town had been a favorite resort of the Roman legions, who built themselves a beautifully functional bath and called the place "Waters of the Sun." Out of the ruins left by the onslaughts of Pict, Scot, Saxon and Dane, a monastery and church had arisen around the mineral springs, which early Christians believed were fed by the tears of fallen angels.

By 1450, the Bishop of Bath was threatening excommunication for mixed, nude wallowing in the tears, and the waters fell heir to the old fertility myth. Attracted by stories of instant pregnancy, the childless Queen Catherine visited seventeenth-century Bath in the hope of soaking up enough fecundity to present Charles II with at least one legitimate offspring to counterbalance the merry monarch's ever-increasing brood of bastards. Though Catherine's mission failed, the publicity of the royal visit attracted a cross section of aristocracy, social climbers, gamblers and gay ladies that made Bath the birthplace of British café society.

For an impressionistic peep into the mystique of seventeenth-century bathing we are indebted, appropriately enough, to Samuel Pepys, who visited the baths at Bath in June of 1667: "Up at four o'clock, being by appointment called up to the Cross Bath, where we were carried one after another . . . And by and by, though we designed to have done before company come, much company come; very fine ladies; and the manner pretty enough, only methinks it cannot be clean to go so many bodies together in the same water. Good conversation among them that are acquainted here, and stay together. Strange to see how hot the water is . . . Carried away, wrapped in a sheet, and in a chair, home; and there one after another thus carried; I staying above two hours in the water, home to bed, sweating for an hour; and by and by, comes musick to play to me, extraordinary good as ever I heard at London almost . . ."

The chummy social atmosphere Pepys describes suggests a trend away from the purely medicinal bathing of the previous century, when the Cross Bath was reportedly "much frequented of People diseased with Lepre, Pokkes, Scabbes and great Aches." That the trend was modest in every respect we learn from Celia Feinnes, a diarist contemporary with Pepys: "The Laydes goes into the bath with garments made of fine yellow canvas, which is stiff and made large with great sleeves like a parson's gown; the water fills it up so that it's borne off that your shape is not seen . . . The gentlemen have drawers and waistcoats of the same sort of canvas, this is the best linning, for the bath water will change any other sort yellow."

A little more than a decade later, soggy gowns, canvas drawers and much of the old decorum seem to have been abandoned, and the author of the highly sensational *A Step to the Bath* was moved to declare in 1700: "Here is perform'd all the Wanton Dalliances imaginable; celebrated beauties, Panting Breasts, and Curious Shapes, almost Expos'd to Publick View; Languishing eyes, Darting Killing Glances, Tempting Amorous Postures, attended by soft Musick, enough to provoke a *Vestal* to forbidden Pleasure, captivate a Saint, and charm a *Jove* . . ." Going a step further, another observer concurred: "The Baths were like so many Bear Gardens, and Modesty was entirely shut out of them. People of both Sexes bathing Day and Night naked; and Dogs, Cats, and even human creatures were hurl'd over the rails, while People were bathing in it."

Although the municipality passed an ordinance against "smoaking Tobacco in bathing Cisterns, singing songs and such disturbances," it had no regulations regarding gambling, and rakes of all ranks and stations wagered freely at cards, dice, cockfights and bowling. Usually, our *Step to the Bath* informant reports, "the Citizens won the Courtiers' money, and the Courtiers swore to be Reveng'd upon their Wives and Daughters."

The literature of Bath abounds in evidence that such revenge was easy for courtier and citizen alike. In *The Bath Unmask'd*, a popular period play, Pander boasts to Sprightly: "As for Ladies—we have all Degrees, as their several Interests draw 'em hither. Those of the first Rank

. . . who Understand the Use of Nature better than to be confin'd to conjugal Constancy, improve their talents by private Intercourse; Coquettes enlarge their Conquests; Prudes indulge in a Corner, and are demure in Publick . . . Profess'd Ladies of Pleasure find Cullies in Abundance . . ."

With the election of the elegant and potbellied Beau Nash as Master of Ceremonies and King of Bath, the town began to assume a veneer of fashionable respectability. Order was restored to the "bathing Cisterns," rules of dress and etiquette were established, gambling was put on a house-controlled basis—and Bath became the leading English resort of the eighteenth century. Its supremacy remained unchallenged until 1789, when the court of George III began to sojourn at seaside Weymouth, where, Fanny Burney reported, "The King bathes and with great success; a machine follows the Royal one into the sea filled with fiddlers who play 'God save the King' as His Majesty takes his plunge."

Whether at Weymouth or Bath, when the season ended, peers, fortune hunters, gamblers and mistresses returned to town for a winter of powdered wigs and perfunctory washing. In the better English homes, mirrored washstands were not unknown and private water companies supplied wealthy Londoners with piped-in water for three hours a day. A curved and shallow bathtub made its appearance in France, concealed in a chaise longue. But, as Siegfried Giedion, a painstaking student of plumbing and people, observed after a study of old French engravings: "Cleanliness of the body could hardly have been its purpose. It forms the background for a scene between a gallant, a young woman, and a procuress. Bath and sin were one."

In 1710, a scene between one such gallant and the modish Mme. de Prie occasioned the first public mention of a new bath-type convenience—the bidet. Seated upon a handsomely wrought boudoir model, Madame was pleased to receive a call from the Marquis d'Argenson, who professed surprise and delight at the sight of the droll little bowl. Advertised by one perplexed merchant of the era as "a porcelain violin case," this aid to feminine daintiness has since become a standard fixture in Continental bathrooms, though guardians of Anglo-American morals have long considered it too French—and, therefore, naughty—for any English-speaking purpose.

The quaint Gallic custom of receiving guests while seated upon a *chaise d'affaires* did not originate with Mme. de Prie, however. Louis XIV regularly gave audience to ambassadors and other favored dignitaries while seated upon the royal close stool and was thus enthroned when he announced his engagement to Mme. de Maintenon. This was known as "French courtesy" and was not to be confused with the Scotch courtesy of shouting "Gardy loo!" ("*Gardez l'eau!*" or "Look out for the water!") before emptying a chamber pot out of an Edinburgh window.

During most of the eighteenth century the call of nature continued to be answered by chamber pots, which were sometimes concealed in sets of dummy books bearing such titles as *Mystères de Paris* and *Voyage to the Low Countries*. Under their carriage seats, my English lord and lady kept traveling versions of the same ceramic necessity—often so arranged that by lifting the seat cushion the interior of the coach could be converted into a mobile privy.

Since Queen Anne's day, Windsor Castle had boasted "a seat of Easement of Marble, with sluices of water" and inventors had been at work on new improvements. Because Harington's metamorphosed jakes had, apparently, been forgotten, the first patented W.C. didn't appear until 1775. Designed by a Bond Street watchmaker, this fully automatic model found a fair degree of acceptance and was soon being installed in London town houses—usually under the stairs or in some windowless closet, where the accumulation of sewer gas was frequently strong enough to fell the proud homeowner and explode at the touch of a lighted candle. A major breakthrough came in 1782, however, when an English cook was credited with "the invention of an entire new machine, a stink trap," which would "entirely prevent the very disagreeable smells from drains and sewers."

Oddly enough, the challenge of inventing a better sewer trap never seemed to stimulate the genius of Benjamin Franklin, although the practical-minded Philadelphian was an accomplished bather and swimmer and had devised a set of hand paddles and foot fins that anticipated the modern frogman's equipment by 200 years. Equally noteworthy is a letter written from London in 1768, in which Franklin confides that to avoid the shock of cold water, "I have found it much more agreeable to my constitution to bathe in another element, I mean cold air. With this view I rise almost every morning and sit in my chamber without any clothes whatever, half an hour or an hour according to the season either reading or writing."

While such scholarly stripping might serve to establish Franklin as an early American nudist, it bespeaks more eloquently the spread of Rousseau's back-to-nature philosophy. In the name of "the noble savage," bodily vigor was given a vogue that carried over into the nineteenth century, when, under the guidance of the physical culturist Priessnitz, naked Austrian aristocrats frisked through their native pine forests and bathed under jets of icy mountain water.

Aristocratic British travelers, meanwhile, were becoming more and more beguiled by the pleasures of the Islamic baths, or *hammams*. Their accounts glowed with poetic enthusiasm. "It was ecstatic enjoyment, it was Elysium, nothing seemed wanting to perfect bliss," one freshly-bathed adventurer rhapsodized. Lady Mary Wortley Montagu (whose grimy hands were considered remarkable even by the French) attended a wedding reception at "one of the finest baths in Constantinople," where the young bridesmaids "appeared without other ornament or covering than their own long hair braided with pearl or ribbon . . . 'Tis not easy to represent to you the beauty of the sight," she concluded, "most of them being well proportioned and white skinned; all of them perfectly smooth and polished by frequent use of bathing."

On the strength of such reports, enterprising English promoters opened a group of Turkish-style "hummums" in London, but the eight-shilling admission price was well beyond the means of the average Englishman. When the celebrated Italian amorist Casanova visited the city during the latter half of the eighteenth century, he found the Anglo-Oriental attractions of a certain well-known "hummum" in Long Acre an absolute bargain, however. "I also visited the bagnios," he wrote, "where a rich man can sup, bathe and sleep with a fashionable courtesan, of which species there are many in London. It makes a magnificent debauch and only costs six guineas."

From Russia, another traveler reported that the natives "find the use of the bath acts as a powerful remedy in carrying off the superabundant humours. Scores of individuals mingle together in a heated apartment, and after being sweated, switched, and half-boiled, rush into the open air like so many frantic satyrs and *plunge into the coldest water*."

The Abbé Chappe d'Auteroche, who visited Tobolsk to witness an eclipse of Venus, also managed to take a long look at the exotic public baths. "These are shared by men and women alike," he noted. "Planks partition the sexes, but since both sexes leave the bath naked, they see one another in this condition and stand conversing upon the most indifferent matters. In the poorer villages the sexes use the baths promiscuously."

The Finnish bath, or *sauna*, was almost identical with that of the Russians, and turn-of-the-century tourists found the friendly Finns willing "to leave the Bath, and assist in yoking or unyoking, or fetching provender for horses, or in anything else, without any sort of covering whatever, while the passengers sit shivering with cold, though wrapped up in a good sound wolf's skin."

Northern nudity and hospitality aside, British hygienists were concerned with establishing national norms of cleanliness and sanitation. When Victoria took the throne in 1837, Windsor Castle was plagued with fifty-three overflowing cesspools. There were no baths at all in Buckingham Palace at the time of her coronation, and those of her subjects who thought such matters important made do with portable hip baths that had to be filled by hand. Reformers raised their voices against this deplorable lag in basic hygiene. "We must have a standard of cleanliness as well as of truth," David Urquhart pleaded. "We must look for one tested by long experience and fixed from ancient days—this is The Bath."

The Bath, as Urquhart saw it, was nothing less than the complete Islamic treatment, with its emphasis upon cleansing the pores from within by means of perspiration as well as from without by means of soap and water. It was Urquhart who named it the "Turkish Bath," and it was he who led the fight for the building of two large public baths in London—fitted, of course, with private cubicles where proper Victorians could sweat in seemly solitude.

While the English were admiring their modest Turkish delights, the Irish were pointing with pride to their own ancient "sweating houses"—beehive structures of stone, similar to outdoor ovens, in which Erin's kings and countrymen had been sweating themselves since the days of Finn Mac Cool. In Germany, as a matter of fact, the Turkish Bath was known as the Irish Bath. When the first such establishments were opened in America, they were advertised variously as Turkish, Russian and

Greek—though they might just as well have been called Indian, since sweat huts had been used by all native tribes as a cure for colds, fevers and other maladies. "Their *Physick*," according to Cotton Mather, "is, excepting a few odd *Specificks*, which some of them Encounter certain Cases with, nothing hardly, but an *Hot-House*, or a *Powaw* [medicine man]; their *Hot-House* is a little *Cave* about eight foot over, where after they have terribly heated it, a Crew of them go sit and sweat and smoke for an Hour together, and then immediately run into some very cold adjacent Brook, without the least Mischief to them; 'tis this way they recover themselves from some Diseases, particularly from the French," which is nowadays known as syphilis.

With the growth of egalitarian and hygienic ideals during the nineteenth century, socially conscious people began to be troubled by the fact that a proper steam bath could be enjoyed only by those who could afford a visit to a specially constructed building. To answer the need for simpler and more available facilities, European hygienists began promoting the now-familiar shower, or "rain bath," in the early 1830's. But the novelty of a mild needle spray was so great that after three decades a French practitioner found it "no rare thing to see a subject who at this first shower betrays actual terror, shouts, struggles, runs away, experiences frightening suffocation and palpitation."

Since human beings are remarkably adaptable, only two more decades went by before Dr. Oscar Lasser could triumphantly declare, "*Die Douche als Volksbad!*" ("The Rain Bath is the People's Bath!") During the latter half of the century, portable showers had found their way into many English homes by virtue of their popularity among army officers who had served in the tropics. Visiting Americans fancied the overhead sprinkler and introduced it into this country, where it has since rivaled the tub as the number-one body cleanser of a busy, no-nonsense nation.

Unfortunately for students of the history of the American bath, virtually all available references repeat a group of bogus facts perpetrated by the late H. L. Mencken in 1926. In one of his more elephantine moods of intellectual superiority, Mencken wrote and published a brief history of the bathtub which he later admitted to be a complete fabrication. "I alleged," he finally confessed, "that the bathtub was unknown in the New World until the 40's of the last century, and that it was then invented in Cincinnati. I described how the inventor, in the absence of running water in the town, employed Aframericans to haul it up from the Ohio river in buckets. I told how a tub was put into the White House in the 50's, and how Millard Fillmore took the first presidential bath. I ended by saying that medical men of the United States unanimously opposed the new invention as dangerous to health, and that laws against it were passed in Massachusetts and Pennsylvania."

For almost nine years Mencken enjoyed the peculiar satisfaction of having deceived his readers while the spurious facts were reprinted in books, magazines, encyclopedias, newspaper columns and syndicated feature stories. Because of this so-called "Bathtub Hoax," the entire record has been made suspect, and at least one President of the United States—Harry S. Truman—was unwittingly duped into repeating Mencken's fantasies as interesting footnotes to the history of the White House.

There are claims that stationary tubs were first installed in a group of Philadelphia row houses in 1832, but it's safe to say that the modern combination of tub, toilet and basin was not to be found in many American homes before the 1890's. The saga of the American bathroom, then, is scarcely seventy-five years old. With the passing of early prestige-symbol types—with their mahogany-enclosed tubs, gold and silver faucets, and sculptured toilet bowls—the pageant of private plumbing moved steadily in the direction of the functional. The tub was recessed into the tiled floor, the toilet tank was lowered from the ceiling, the faucets were plated with nontarnishing chrome, and the shower was installed in its own efficient cell. Barring fanciful guest towels, novelty bath mats and poodle-cute slipcovers for the john lid, the room has been stripped for the speedy performance of a few essential operations. The door can be locked against intruders, the toilet is designed for single occupancy, and the tub and shower are sleek one-passenger jobs in which we can soak or scrub in the innocent belief that the sole purpose of the bath is—and ever has been—to get clean.

At the moment, privacy is still the keynote and there are no signs of an immediate return to musicians, Mamelukes or "trim waitresses" to scrub one's back. But in recent years a small drift toward a kind of clubby elegance has been evidenced in custom-built accommodations featuring twin tubs, washbasins and toilets to match His and Her towels. Wall-to-wall carpeting, gold-plated faucets, steam-bath stalls, scented shower heads and pink porcelain bidets all figure in luxury-class lavatory designs, together with marble telephones, built-in sun lamps and roomy, rectangular tubs in which any number can splash and play.

It should be noted, moreover, that a definite trend to social bathing is under way amongst the increasing numbers of Americans who have experienced the invigorating effects of the now-fashionable Finnish sauna. "What started here fourteen years ago as a recherché European oddity is fast becoming a genuine bit of Americana," Priscilla Tucker observed in a 1964 report on the sweat-and-plunge phenomenon which appeared in the New York *Herald Tribune.* "People are sauna-ing together all over the place," she declared. "We have pioneered the pre-fab sauna, the housing development sauna, the motel sauna, the executive sauna, the pre-cocktail sauna, and the hairdresser sauna."

Like the Abbé Chappe d'Auteroche, who eyewitnessed the coed bathing accommodations of old Russia, Miss Tucker went out to check the facts for herself. She visited a Manhattan beauty salon and found the fair customers "sitting around the sauna hut with other naked ladies not of their acquaintance." She looked in at a sauna cottage at Sugarbush, where the ski set practices sweating and soaking "as a bracer for the cocktail hour," and journeyed to suburban New Rochelle to inspect a Sauna Fun House that boasted a large redwood sweat hut, Finnish decor, and a bubbling Parisian Plunge Pool.

According to Miss Tucker, the sauna-ing suburbanites

have wisely eschewed the old Finnish custom of beating each other with birch-twig switches to stimulate circulation—a practice that might easily get out of hand in communities where emotions regarding zoning amendments, tax assessments and the P.T.A. are apt to run rather high. One gathered, too, that the water in the Parisian Plunge Pool was considerably warmer than that in the Gulf of Finland—and that it wasn't very likely that the hospitable natives of New Rochelle would ever go so far as to leave their overheated Fun House in dead of winter to welcome the shivering motorist. But in some areas, at least, there are indications that the home sauna may eventually replace the back-yard swimming pool as a suburban status symbol.

Sensing the possibility of a change toward more sociable bathing habits, one American manufacturer of bathroom fixtures is said to be selling the idea that "The family that bathes together stays together"—a slogan which some intensely gregarious homebodies may find irresistible, suggesting as it does the close-knit warmth and solidarity of family life that has traditionally existed among such group-bathing peoples as the Japanese. But many togetherness-weary Americans, to whom the bathroom represents the last stronghold of privacy in an increasingly doorless world of "open-floor" plans, glass walls and skimpy room dividers, can be expected to react to this new sales pitch with shouts, struggles, palpitation, and other symptoms of terror.

As of today, of course, it's impossible to say which faction will ultimately prevail. But in light of the fact that dining, living and sleeping areas have successfully supplanted the rooms which were once devoted to such purposes, it would be foolhardy to rule out the possibility that the American bathroom may be one day metamorphosed into a bathroom area—a doorless, wall-less grouping of decorator-designed conveniences: a communal tub, peekaboo plumbing, free-form seats and a through-view from the street.

Fortunately, as long as the freedom of choice exists, Americans may bathe pretty much as they please. Outgoing organization types may tub, shower, sweat and scrub in family groups, friendly twosomes or socially festive platoons, while the solitude-loving loner may still retreat to his tightly locked cubicle to soak, sing and, perhaps, gratefully murmur in paraphrase of Abooseer's Arabian king: "By my head, this house would never be a home, save for the privacy of this Bath!"

IV

TOASTS AND TOASTING

Toasts and Toasting

Curiously enough, it was as a result of bathing in mixed company that Englishmen first began to drink "toasts" —a gracious and well-nigh universal custom which the eighteenth-century wit Richard Brinsley Sheridan gaily hailed as "an excuse for the glass" and the seventeenth century's puritanical William Prynne glumly denounced as "a kind of shoehorn to draw on drink in great abundance."

Tugging on our own merry mukluks and dipping into a few well-aged volumes of liquid lore, we soon learn that most of mankind has traditionally drunk "healths" and that the idea of drinking a "toast" is peculiar to those who quaff and converse in English.

As a matter of sober fact, even the English drank nothing but healths until the latter part of the seventeenth century. Prior to that time, a "toast" was only a slice of lightly browned bread which people ate for breakfast, just as they do today—with the singular exception that a bit of toast was often floated in a tankard or bowl of warm spiced ale to provide a morsel of nourishment at a time when individual serving plates were scarce and costly. This once highly practical custom of adding such foods as toast, raw eggs and roasted apples to beer and ale is reflected in the modern habit of dressing up drinks with olives, cherries and little pickled onions, and the practice persisted among kings, courtiers and common folk long after the English had acquired enough plates and tableware to serve a meal in style.

In the earliest historical account of how the word "toast" came to be associated with the ritual of drinking to someone's health, essayist Richard Steele reported in 1709 that the expression first came into vogue among the hard-drinking blue bloods of the Restoration, who were wont to resort to the city of Bath to soak up the fashionable mineral waters in an atmosphere of wine, women and whist. "It happened," as Steele explained in *The Tatler*, "that on a publick Day a celebrated Beauty of those Times was in the Cross Bath, and one of the Crowd of her Admirers took a Glass of the Water in which the Fair one stood, and drank her Health to the Company. There was in the Place a gay Fellow, half-fuddled, who offered to jump in, and swore, Tho' he liked not the Liquor, he would have the Toast. He was opposed in his Resolution; yet this whim gave Foundation to the present Honour which is done to the Lady we mention in our Liquors, who has ever since been called a Toast."

According to the eleventh Edition of the *Encyclopaedia Britannica*, the "custom of drinking 'health' to the living is probably derived from the ancient religious rite of drinking to the gods and the dead. The Greeks and Romans at meals poured out libations to their gods, and at ceremonial banquets drank to them . . ." In distilling this information down into a couple of quick verbal jiggers, the *Britannica* allows several essential facts to evaporate, however. In a libation, for example, a given quantity of liquor is poured out on the ground as a sacrifice to a deity, while in drinking to someone's health the liquor goes gliding down the drinker's own throat. The Greek and Roman custom of passing around a "cup to the good spirit," furthermore, is believed to have originated with the "cup of salvation" which was religiously quaffed by the ancient Hebrews, whose drinking vessels were often smashed on the ground to prevent their being defiled by secular use—a practice which led to the traditional Jewish wedding custom of shattering a wine glass in remembrance of the destruction of the Holy Temple and the sorrows of exile and persecution.

The custom of raising a glass aloft in honor of the person being toasted is also attributed to the early Greeks, who were wine-guzzling health addicts of heroic capacity. At least three devotional toasts were offered to the gods at dinner, and these were followed by healths drunk in honor of the host, individual guests, guardian deities, and friends both living and dead. In the words of one nineteenth-century authority on ancient Athenian drinking habits, "They drank not only deeply, but progressively so; their last cup at parting was the largest, and went by the terrible name of *the cup of necessity*"—which, reduced to more moderate proportions, became our "one for the road."

Grecian toasting goblets, which were carried by cupbearers from one reclining guest to the next, were often of prodigious size and are the ancient prototype of the large trophy cups awarded to winners of modern yacht races and other sporting events. Smaller, individual cups were generally used for performing the morning drinking rite, whose name was synonymous with "breakfast," and for offering the bedtime toast to Hermes, with which the health-happy Hellenes concluded each day—thus setting a pleasantly woozy precedent for our own relaxing "nightcap."

"Nothing in Nature's sober found," the poet Anacreon sang, in expressing the Athenian world view *circa* 500 B.C., "But an eternal Health goes round."

Fill up the Bowl then, fill it high
Fill all the Glasses there; for why
Should every Creature drink but I?
Why, Men of Morals, tell me why?

Though temperate by Anacreon's standards, most Grecian men of morals and philosophy were themselves fairly accomplished drinkers, as the American novelist Owen Wister once suggested in a quatrain calculated to make the classical scholar hoist a glass in grief:

Said Aristotle unto Plato,
"Have another sweet potato?"
Said Plato unto Aristotle,
"Thank you, I prefer the bottle."

In Wister's defense it must be acknowledged that Plato's mentor, Socrates, could drain off a two-quart wine cooler in one long pull and go on tippling and talking till dawn. Indeed, the Athenian tendency to combine serious thinking with heavy drinking is nowhere better exemplified than in Plato's *Symposium,* a book whose very title was derived from *symposian,* the Greek word for a drinking party at which the quaffing of healths was both compulsory and continuous.

So numerous were the toasts required at dinner that Greeks and Romans alike customarily appointed a toastmaster to keep track of the order of healths and decide the quantity to be drunk for each. To the old Greek ritual of drinking to every god in the Parthenon, Roman revelers added a rousing "three times three" in honor of the Graces and Muses and pledged their loyalty to Caesar by downing a cup for each letter in the emperor's name—a stupefying custom which was also employed in toasting each other's mistresses. As Martial described it, "Six cups to Naevia's health go quickly round," and fair Justina must be honored with an additional seven.

One English historian maintains that it was the Roman conquerors who taught ancient Britons "to drink healths to the Emperor, and to toast the reigning belles with brimming bumpers." Actually, though, the Romans had very little to teach the booze-thirsty barbarians of the

North, who had been belting down liquid tributes to gods, chieftains, kinsmen and chums since the prehistoric discovery that the fermentation of honeycombs in water would produce a kind of beer called "mead." The Norse Valhalla, for instance, was hardly more than a heavenly beer hall where the spirits of deserving heroes drank healths through all eternity; and one of the most ancient of all toasting terms—"skoal," or *skål*—survives from the grisly and forgotten age when Norse warriors drank victorious toasts from the *skalle*, or "skull," of a slain enemy. In like manner, the English word "health" stems from the Old Norse greeting, *Heill!*—which also gave us "hail," "heal," "hale" and "whole." From the Norsemen's *Ves heill!* or "Be thou well!" came the Anglo-Saxon toast, *Wes hal!*—which the hale-and-hardy English eventually slurred into "wassail," a word usually associated with a brimming bowl of Christmas cheer.

The festive custom of wassailing antedates Christmas by many centuries, however, and is believed to have evolved from the Northerners' midwinter fertility rites, in which bands of boozy celebrants trooped through the forests and made libations of ale, mead or hard cider to restore the dormant fertility of fruit trees. This quaint old pagan practice is said to be still observed in some tradition-rich rural areas of Britain and was fetchingly described by *The Gentlemen's Magazine* as part of the Twelfth-night ceremonies in Devonshire in 1791:

"On the Eve of the Epiphany, the farmer, attended by his workmen, with a large pitcher of cyder, goes to the orchard, and there, encircling one of the best-bearing trees, they drink the following toast three several times:

"Here's to thee old apple tree,
Whence thou may'st bud, and whence
thou may'st blow!
And whence thou may'st bear apples enow!
Hats full!—Caps full!
Bushel-bushel-sacks full!
And my pockets full, too! Huzza!"

In the festivities that usually followed, the farmer and his wife were wassailed with yet another old toasting song:

Here's to our horse, and to his right ear,
God send our measter a happy new year;
A happy new year as e'er he did see—
With my wassailing bowl I drink to thee.

Here's to our mare, and to her right eye,
God send our mistress a good Christmas pie . . .

Whether held on Twelfth-night, New Year's Eve or Christmas Eve, the feast had as its chief feature the bowl of wassail, in which the ancient fruit-and-livestock theme was further evidenced by the addition of roasted crab apples to the brew and the fact that the warm and comforting concoction was affectionately known as "lamb's wool." In a rhymed recipe for this traditional Yuletide treat, the poet Herrick directed seventeenth-century wassailmen to "crown the bowl full with gentle lamb's wooll,"

Adde sugar, nutmeg and ginger,
With store of ale too;
And thus ye must doe,
To make the wassaile a swinger.

Long before Herrick hipped to the ginger-and-apples bit, the pagan toasts of the North Europeans had been adapted to Christian devotions and healths which were once drunk to mythical nature gods were now addressed to the Savior and all the saints and angels. Gallic healths to the Pope were drunk "to the good Father," or *au bon Père*—which the English called drinking "a bumper"—and the old wassailing songs set a joyous precedent for the first Christmas carols—the earliest of which often imposed the obligation to drink or be damned. "Lords, by Christmas and the host of this mansion, hear my toast," the old Norman caroler sang:

Each must drain his cup of wine,
And I the first will toss off mine:
Thus I advise,
Here then I bid you all Wassail,
Cursed be he who will not say Drink hail.

Since no true Christian could refuse to drink to the saints, or the "Christ Mass" which was Christmas, toasting and wassailing soon made drunkenness as obligatory as it had ever been in the heathen days of yore and gore. As early as the fourth century, St. Augustine denounced the "filthy and unhappy custom of drinking healths," which was "but a ceremony and relic of Pagans." But the best vineyards and breweries in all Christendom flourished behind monastery walls, and many of the clergy were so habitually and publicly imbued with the blessings of fermentation that in the eighth century St. Boniface felt compelled to bring the matter to the attention of Archbishop Cuthbert. "In your diocese certain Bishops not only do not hinder drunkenness, but they themselves indulge in excess of drink, and force others to drink till they are intoxicated," Boniface complained. "This is most certainly a great crime for a servant of God to do or to have done . . ."

Distasteful as the idea of tippling monks and fuddled bishops may be to modern churchgoers, it should be recognized that the convivial health-drinking of the clergy brought a touch of civilizing ceremony to the secular drinking bouts of the Dark Ages. Prior to the Christian conversion of Scandinavia, for example, Viking freebooters had the nasty habit of inviting Britons to drink, only in order to cut their throats when they tossed back their heads to drain the proffered beaker—a savage bit of *Skål*-duggery that led to the old English practice of "pledging the health" of a kinsman or friend and standing guard while he drank. Bloody and murderous, too, were the quarrels that broke out among drinkers when one was accused of swigging more than his share from the communal bowl or cup. Under the influence of the clergy, drinkers were organized into fraternal guilds, where brotherhood and mutual aid were pledged from a large "loving cup" in which the portions were measured off by a set of metal pegs.

Though brawling and bloodshed decreased, it soon

became apparent that the new societies merely ensured that members all had an equal chance to get thoroughly stoned, while the practice of "drinking to pegs" resulted in brotherly contests to see who could guzzle the most portions in honor of the patron saint and take his fellows "down a peg" by quaffing a measure more. For this reason, toasting "between pegs" was condemned by the Council of Westminster in 1101 and again at the Latern Council of Innocent III. But despite all decrees and injunctions, monks, monarchs and lushes of lowly station continued to invoke the names of saints and do honor to things sacred in order to guarantee that no toast would be refused. At the court of good King Wenceslaus, the toastmaster commanded all to drink "in the name of the blessed archangel St. Michael"; and more than a century later, no less a protesting monk than Martin Luther cherished a pet drinking mug, "around which were three rings. The first he said represented the Ten Commandments, the second the Apostles' Creed, and the third the Lord's Prayer." Luther, we are told, "was highly amused that he was able to drain the glass of wine through the Lord's Prayer, whereas his friend Agricola could not get beyond the Ten Commandments."

In France the chug-a-lugging churchmen of the sixteenth century were ribaldly satirized by Rabelais, whose own literary toasts were robustly secular and brief: "Luck to you, comrade!" "Drink up, friends: your health, there!" "Hail to all tosspots! Pity the thirsty!" Whether the sentiments were religious or worldly, French and German toasters couldn't begin to match the flamboyance of the royal Danish style which

Shakespeare described in the scene where young Prince Hamlet and his friend Horatio are waiting on the battlements for the Ghost to appear. Startled by the thunder of cannons at midnight, Horatio asks, "What does this mean, my lord?"

HAMLET: The king doth wake to-night and takes his rouse,
Keeps wassail, and the swaggering up-spring reels;
And, as he drains his draughts of Rhenish down,
The kettle-drum and trumpet thus bray out
The triumph of his pledge.

HORATIO: Is it a custom?

HAMLET: Ay, marry, is 't:
But to my mind, though I am native here
And to the manner born, it is a custom
More honour'd in the breach than the observance.
This heavy-headed revel east and west
Makes us traduced and tax'd of other nations: . . .

Hamlet's melancholy estimate of the effects of excessive wassailing in government reflects a like attitude on the part of England's good Queen Bess. As one who could tuck away a quart of ale at breakfast, Elizabeth was no teetotaler; but the continual drinking of courtly toasts often left her counselors too befuddled to be entrusted with affairs of state and prompted her to declare that she never fared worse than when her health was drunk.

Shakespeare's Iago describes the tankard-clanking English as "most potent in their potting; your Dane, your German, and your swag-bellied Hollander, Drink-ho! —are nothing to your English!" Something of this potency is indicated in the Elizabethan custom of toasting *super negulum*, or "on the nail."

Here's a health to Tom Brown,
Drink up your ale without shrinking,
Put a pond on your nail,
And kiss the glass's tail,
And fill it up again without ceasing!

The point was for the drinker to drain his glass at one pull, leaving just enough ale at the bottom "to cover his finger nail, but if he leaves too much, or not enough, the penalty is to drink another"—a jolly little juice-time game that could cause a poor guesser to down a dozen quarts and end up with fingers that smelled "like Brewer's aprons."

"Nor have we one or two kinde of drunkards onely, but eight kindes," Thomas Nash wrote in a period appraisal of the effects of such potting and toasting. "*The first is Ape drunke*, and he leapes, and sings, and hollowes, and daunceth for the heavens: *the second is Lion drunke*, and he flings the pots about the house, calls his Hostesse whore, breaks the glasse windowes with his dagger, and is apt to quarrell with any man that speaks to him: *the third is Swine drunke*, heavy lumpish, and sleepie, and cries for a little more drinke, and a fewe more cloathes: *the fourth is Sheepe drunke*, wise in his own conceipt, when he cannot bring foorth a right word: *the fifth is Mawdlen drunke*, when a fellow will weepe for kindnes in the midst of Ale, and kisse you, saying: 'By God Captaine I love thee, goe thy waies thou dost not thinke so often of me as I do of thee, I would (if it pleased God) I could not love thee as well as I doo,' and then he puts his finger in his eye, and cries: *the sixt is Martin drunke*, when a man is drunke and drinkes himself sober ere he stirre: *the seventh is Goate drunke*, when in his drunkenness he hath no mind but on Lechery: *the eighth is Foxe drunke*, as many of the Dutchmen bee, will never bargaine but when they are drunke.

"All these species and more have I seen practised in one Company at one sitting," Nash avers; and no one who has ever attended an office Christmas party can possibly doubt his claim. Familiar, too, is the morning-after remorse that prompted the following resolution, scrawled on the flyleaf of an old English Bible: "Frome this daye forwarde to the ende of my life, I will never pledge anye health, nor drink a carowse in a glass, cupp, bowle, or any other drinking instrument whatsoever, whosoever it be, or ffrome whomsoever it come. . . ."

Considering the intemperance of the period, literary skoalers may be moved to speculate whether Ben Jonson's classic toast "To Celia" owed its inspiration to the Muse of poetry or the morning-after shakes and megrims:

Drink to me only with thine eyes,
And I will pledge with mine;
Or leave a kiss but in the cup
And I'll not look for wine. . . .

If one can take the word of the English Puritans, neither Jonson's Celia nor any other city belle was likely to be satisfied with an exchange of intoxicating looks and saucy glances, however. In seventeenth-century London there was reputed to be a "multitude" of "sottish women" who would "quaff with the most riotous, and give pledge for pledge." Even more deplorable was the fact that in some parts of England young maidens became so depraved by the unbridled license of Maypole festivities as to "drink healths upon their knees." Kneeling toasts were "vile in men but abominable in women," the puritanical author of *Funebria Florae* fumed; and in this respect at least his sentiments were seconded by that hard-drinking advocate of the eyeball highball—Ben Jonson himself. As a Mermaid Tavern regular and no-frills "cupp-and-bowle" man, Jonson also scorned "such swaggering humours" as the practice of piercing the arm with a dagger and mingling one's blood with wine in order to make a sacrament of drinking the health of a beloved lady.

Among university scholars a fad for toasting women in "some nauseus decoction" paralleled our latter-day panty raids and goldfish swallowing. In describing the drinking customs of seventeenth-century Oxford, one disapproving clergyman tells of a student who drank his mistress's health in wine mixed with a large spoonful of soot. "His companion, determined not to be outdone, brought from his closet a phial of ink, which he drank, exclaiming, 'Io triumphe and Miss Molly!'" According to the same source, these "crack-brained young men also esteemed it a great privilege to get possession of a great beauty's shoe, in order that they might ladle wine out of a bowl down their throats with it, the while they drank to the 'lady of little worth' or the 'light-heeled mistress' who had been its former wearer."

In the light of this fetishistic practice—which nineteenth-century *bon vivants* were to revive with ballerinas' dancing shoes—one can better understand the confusion of a group of seventeenth-century Frenchmen who observed Londoners soaking up healths from the tall leather tankards which the British called "black jacks" and reported that the English "drinke out of their bootes." Judging from an inventory of health-drinkers' hardware published in 1635, the English were indeed likely to drink from anything that didn't leak: "Of drinking cups divers and sundry sorts we have, some of elme, some of box, some of holly, &c. Mazers, broad-mouthed dishes, noggins, whiskins, crinzes, ale-bowles, wassel-bowles, court-dishes, tankards, kannes, from a pottle to a pint, from a pint to a gill. . . .We have besides cups made of hornes of beasts, of cocker nuts, of goords, of the eggs of estriches; others made of the shells of divers fishes brought from the Indies and other places, and shining like mother of pearle. Every taverne can afford you flat bowles, French bowles, bonnet cups, beare bowles, beakers; and private householders can furnish their cupboards with flagons, tankards, beere cups, wine bowles, some white, some percell guilt, some guilt all over."

To the modern chronicler of "pottles," "kannes" and "cocker-nut" cups, the period spelling of "guilt" for "gilt" might almost seem a Freudian error born of the English Puritans' wrathful condemnation of the "worldly, carnall, prophane, nay heathenish and devillish custome" of drinking healths. The fact that health-drinking could also be murderous led to the widespread use of glass-bottomed tankards that enabled a tavern patron to keep an eye out for potential cutthroats while in the highly vulnerable position of draining off a pint. This, in turn, supposedly led to the use of the phrase, "Here's looking at you"—a friendly word of warning that has since become one of our most familiar toasts.

It is mainly to antitoasting tracts, such as William Prynne's *Health's Sicknesse* and Gascoigne's *Delicate Dyet for Daintie mouthed Droonkards*, that one must turn for information concerning the conspicuous cupmanship of the period. For a detailed account of the manner in which a health was drunk in the days of the first King James, for instance, there is no better report than that of the pietistic scribbling squire, Richard Brathwaite, whose descriptions of Stuart pub life were written under the not-so-sober sobriquet of "Drunken Barnabee": "He that beginnes a health hath his prescribed orders; first uncovering the head he takes a full cup in his hand, and setting his countenance with grave aspect, he craves an audience; silence being once obtained, he begins to breathe out the name peradventure of some honourable personage that was worthy of a better regard than to have his name polluted at so unfitting a time, amongst a company of drunkards, but his health is drunk to, and he that pledges must likewise off with his cap, kisse his fingers, and bow himself in sign of reverent acceptance. When the leader sees his follower thus prepared, he sups up his breath, turnes the bottom of his cup upward, and in ostentation of his dexteritie gives the cup a phillip to make it cry *twange*, and thus the first scene is acted."

During the reigns of James I and his son, Charles, fingers were kissed and tankards were flipped to the health of the king at tavern meetings between friends and at meals in humble cottages. But for all the toasts drunk to his health, Charles I fared far worse than Elizabeth. When, at last, the elegant Stuart lost his head to the ax of the Puritans in 1649, the drinking of healths was forbidden by law and the jolly wassail bowl was outlawed, together with all the other "heathenish" trappings of Yuletide.

Though the celebration of Christmas was sanctimoniously avoided in Puritan New England, the "Saints" of Massachusetts displayed a most decided preference for beer over water and were not above drinking a health whenever it suited their purpose. While excessive drinking was discouraged and punished, New England fanaticism was never as well organized as that of the puritanical Scots of Fife, who, in 1650, established a special morals squad "to take notice of all disorderly walkers . . . swearers, haunters of ale-houses, especially at unreasonable hours and long sitters there and drinkers of healths."

Chief among the "long sitters" of London were those

monarchists who had escaped the vindictiveness of Cromwell's Puritan government to gather in royalist taverns and drink subversive toasts to exiled Charles II. Eleven long years went down the hatch before Charles was restored to the throne in 1660, when an outbreak of riotous royalist health-drinking caused the merry monarch to issue a troubled "Proclamation against Prophaneness." Fun was fun, the far-from-prudish Charles acknowledged, but there was "a set of men of whom we have heard much, and are sufficiently ashamed, who spend their time in taverns, tippling houses, and debauches, giving no other evidence of affection for us but in drinking our health, and inveighing against all others who are not of their own dissolute temper."

Round-the-clock toasting and drunkenness, committed in the king's name, had already forced Louis XIV to suspend all "wine courtesies" at the French court. But Charles's proclamation seems to have been addressed solely to lower-class tosspots, for no tavern or tippling house could boast a more dissolute group of health-drinkers than the royal court of England. Palace gallants revived the old Roman custom of drinking a cup for each letter in a lady's name, and Charles himself was reported to have drunk a boozy *rapprochement* with his estranged brother, the Duke of York, upon his royal knees—after which, according to Samuel Pepys, the whole party "fell a-crying for joy, being all maudlin and kissing one another, the King the Duke of York, the Duke of York the King, and in such a maudlin pickle as never people were; and so passed the day."

The Stuart pickle was reportedly compounded when

Charles stood to respond to a toast in the officers' mess of a Royal Navy vessel and bumped his head on a low beam with such force that he immediately sank into his seat again—a most painful and mortifying mishap that supposedly started a new tradition for drinking toasts while sitting down. But the story is cast in doubt by yet another entry in Pepys' *Diary*, where an eminent Puritan divine, named "Silver-Tongued" Bates, is described as notable for his "singularity in not rising nor drinking the King's nor other healths at the table." This would seem to suggest the possibility, at least, that the decline in pop-up toasting may have resulted simply from a Puritan reluctance to honor earthly rulers, combined with the growth of libertarian ideas among a rising middle class whose first loyalty was to property and trade.

Considering the quantities of ale, beer and wine consumed in drinking seventeenth-century toasts, sitting and kneeling may well have been more a matter of necessity than of choice or accident. At the wedding reception for Lady Ross in 1693, "all the guests proceeded to the great hall, where a *great cistern* of sack posset was discovered, and at once began the drinking of healths, by old and young alike, at first in spoons, and afterwards in silver cups." And when Charles's brother, the Duke of York, was proclaimed King James II in 1685, his health was publicly drunk in glasses three feet long—the so-called "yard of ale" that is still served in traditional trumpet-shaped glasses at Ye Olde Cheshire Cheese tavern in London.

James II fared badly, too, despite the healths which were drunk in his name. Deposed after three turbulent years, he fled to France, and the throne fell to the Prince of Orange, who became William III and introduced the English to the potency and economy of Holland gin. In the restless and rowdy period that followed, Jacobites who favored the return of James drank seemingly loyal toasts "to the King" by placing a bowl of water on the table between them to signify that they were secretly drinking to the exiled James, the king "over the water." While England teetered on the brink of civil war, political "mug clubs" were formed in order for Jacobites and anti-Jacobites to drink their partisan toasts without fear of bloodshed or reprisal. When the parties later evolved into Tory and Whig, the mug clubs became the leading political and social groups of London. Easily the most illustrious was the famed Kit-cat Club, whose membership included such Whiggish wits and worthies as the Duke of Marlborough, Sir Robert Walpole, Congreve, Vanbrugh, Addison and Steele. It is to the Kit-cat playwright and architect, John Vanbrugh, that we owe the booziest toasting scene of the period theater. The play is *The Provok'd Wife*, and the scene is laid in the Blue Posts tavern, where Lord Rake, Sir John Brute, Colonel Bully and others of like alcoholic ilk "are discovered at a table, drinking" in preparation for a night on the town:

LORD RAKE: Come, boys, charge again — So — Confusion to all order! Here's liberty of conscience!

ALL: Huzza!

LORD RAKE: I'll sing you a song I made this morning to this purpose.

The song, which exalts the liberty of conscience to be found in a bottle over the limited freedoms offered by the king and state, ends in a tribute to the guilt-free hedonism that was characteristic of the late seventeenth century:

> *No saucy remorse*
> *Intrudes in my course,*
> *No impertinent notions of evil;*
> *So there's claret in store,*
> *In peace I've my whore*
> *And in peace I jog on to the devil.*

"But drink away," Lord Rake urges, hoisting his cup aloft; "the night steals upon us; we shall want time to be lewd in . . . Now let the spirit of clary go round. Fill me a brimmer. Here's to our forlorn hope. — Courage, knight; victory attends you."

SIR JOHN BRUTE: And laurels shall crown me; drink away, and be damn'd.

LORD RAKE: Again, boys; t' other glass, and damn morality.

SIR JOHN BRUTE: Ay—damn morality!—and damn the watch!—and let the constable be married!

ALL: Huzza!

The scene ends with a toast to "Liberty and property!"—a phrase, borrowed from the philosopher John Locke, which was to echo down the following decades as the favorite toast of British Whig reformers and

American revolutionaries. But, as in all other periods and lands, the most compelling reason for a toast was still a woman. At meetings of the Kit-cat Club healths were drunk to the reigning beauty, who was elected each year. "The Manner of her Inauguration is much like that of a Doge in Venice . . ." Steele reported in his *Tatler* article on toasts. "When she is regularly chosen, her Name is written with a Diamond on a Drinking-glass. The Hieroglyphick of the Diamond is to shew her that her Value is imaginary; and that of the Glass to acquaint her that her Condition is frail, and depends on the Hand which holds her." The Kit-cat Club, as one old rhyme alleged, took its name not from any "trim beaux,"

Grey statesmen or green wits
But from its pell-mell pack of toasts,
To old Cats and young Kits.

In the early eighteenth century, the loyal toasts of Englishmen, at home and abroad, were offered to the health of middle-aged Queen Anne. It was on the occasion of the queen's birthday in the year 1714 that Samuel Sewall, then justice of the Superior Court of Massachusetts, was roused from his fireside at the ungodly hour of nine P.M. to quell "the Disorders at the Tavern at the Southend." Arriving at the house in question with a constable and party of three, Sewall found "much Company" who "refus'd to go away." They said they were there "to drink the Queen's Health," he confided to his sympathetic diary, "and thay had many other Healths to drink. Call'd for more Drink: drank to me, and I took notice of the Affront . . . Mr. John Netmaker drank the Queen's Health to me. I told him I drank none; upon that he ceas'd. Mr. Brinley put on his Hat to affront me. I made him take it off. I threaten'd to send some of them to prison; that did not move them. . . . Not having Pen and Ink, I went to take their Names with my Pensil, and not knowing how to Spell their Names, they themselves of their own accord writ them. Mr. Netmaker, reproaching the Province, said they had not made one good Law."

Mr. Netmaker and his health-quaffing cronies were sentenced to pay a fine of five shillings each—a mild enough penalty by the older Puritan standards. But Samuel Sewall was still burdened by his self-confessed error in condemning the many innocent victims of the Salem witch trials in 1692. A man of disturbingly human contrasts, he was also the author of the first plea against Negro slavery to be published in the colonies and a determined wooer of comely widows. Though he refused to drink the health of Queen Anne, he often drank wine with Mrs. Denison and exchanged amorous courtesies of the glass with Madam Winthrop: "She drank to me, I to her . . . She had talk'd of Canary, her Kisses were to me better than the best Canary. . . . "

Imported canary wine was too high-line for the purses of most colonial Americans, who drank their toasts with a variety of homemade brews. There were hard cider and metheglin (made of honey, yeast and water), perry (made from pears) and peachy (made from peaches). Other alcoholic curiosities were made from leaves, bark, berries, beans, roots and cornstalks. In an old sing-along favorite, the courageous Colonists proudly claimed:

Oh, we can make liquor to sweeten our lips
Of pumpkins, of parsnips, of walnut-tree chips.

Gourds and coconut shells supplemented bowls, beakers and tankards as basic equipment for the drinking of colonial healths. But "there was no attempt made to give separate drinking cups of any kind to each individual at the table," Alice M. Earle, the author of *Home Life in Colonial Days,* noted at the close of the last century. "Even when tumbler-shaped glasses were seen in many houses . . . they were of communal size—some held a gallon—and all drank from the same glass. The great punch bowl, not a very handy vessel to handle when filled with punch, was passed up and down as freely as though it were a loving cup, and all drank from its brim. . . ."

At Harvard and Yale this was the original college bowl game, later immortalized by a Dartmouth man in the "Hanover Winter Song": "Ho, a song by the fire! (Pass the pipes, fill the bowl!) Ho, a song by the fire! With a Skoal. . . ." Sarah Kemble Knight, who was said to be Benjamin Franklin's old schoolteacher, watched the communal cup go round a Yankee tavern board and described the drinkers as "being tyed by the Lipps to a pewter engine." Her star pupil, the Sage of Philadelphia himself, referred to the glass-passing custom in an original "Drinking Song" dedicated to the proposition "That Virtue & Safety in Wine-bibbing's found,"

While all that drink Water deserve to be drown'd.
So for Safety & Honesty put the Glass round.

A few decades later, the American toast was not "Safety & Honesty" drunk in mellow wine but "Liberty and property" drunk in the fiery New England rum that was the alcoholic embodiment of the Spirit of '76. As Catherine Drinker Bowen has pointed out in her study of *John Adams and the American Revolution*, "Liberty and property" were the passwords of the entire American rebellion. "Liberty and property were synonymous. . . . What a man owned was his, as his soul was his. No prince, no king, no parliament could take it from him without his consent . . . "

In virtually every small village the symbolic "liberty pole" was planted outside a tavern which served as headquarters for the Sons of Liberty, whose early toasts were a peculiar mixture of the loyal and the rebellious. When members of the Boston group met at Chase's Distillery in 1769 to celebrate the anniversary of Boston's protest to the Stamp Act, forty-five toasts were drunk, commencing with "the King and Queen" and ending with the threat of "Strong halters, firm blocks and sharp axes to all such as deserve either!"

In the opinion of the majority, the man most deserving of sharp axes was none other than Governor Bernard, the king's representative in the Province of Massachusetts, who was credited with having introduced a toasting song that was a favorite with American Tories:

Here's a health to all those that we love,
Here's a health to all those that love us,
Here's a health to all those that love them that love those
That love those that love them that love us.

To the modern American drinker this insidious little tongue twister seems sufficient cause for rebellion in itself. In the light of such repeated provocations, we can only marvel at the restraint of those planter-patriots who, upon the dissolution of the Virginia House of Burgesses by the crown, retired to the Raleigh Tavern in Williamsburg to drink loyal toasts to the king, the royal family, "The Farmer" and a "Speedy and Lasting Union between Great Britain and her Colonies." The bar tab, which came to 32 shillings 9 pence, was picked up by a committeeman who was understandably destined to become "first in the hearts of his countrymen"—George Washington. "It was," according to his biographer, Francis Rufus Bellamy, "his first expenditure for liberty."

In 1777—when the embattled Americans were hoisting their mugs of rum grog with shouts of "Death to the tyrant!" and "Freedom forever!"—Richard Brinsley Sheridan attended the London opening of his brilliant new comedy, *The Rivals,* and heard Sir Harry Bumper sing one of the merriest toasting songs that the wit of an Englishman had ever devised:

Here's to the maiden of bashful fifteen;
Here's to the widow of fifty;
Here's to the flaunting extravagant quean,
And here's to the housewife that's thrifty.

CHORUS: Let the toast pass—
Drink to the lass,
I'll warrent she'll prove an excuse for the glass.

Here's to the charmer whose dimples we prize;
Now to the maid who has none, sir;
Here's to the girl with a pair of blue eyes,
And here's to the nymph with but one, sir.

Whether slim or clumsy, white-bosomed or brown-skinned, any woman could, in short, be toasted with a bumper and thus provide "an excuse for the glass." But in October, 1781, a more momentous excuse was offered by the surrender of the British forces at Yorktown, which brought the American Revolution to a close. General Washington and Rochambeau, commander of the French allies, sat down to dinner with the defeated Lord Cornwallis and his officers. Rochambeau raised his glass "To the United States!" Washington responded with a health "To the King of France!" Cornwallis, with the air of a man playing a verbal trump, pointedly proposed a toast "To the King!" "Of England!" Washington quickly qualified. "Confine him there and I'll drink him a full bumper!"

No event in American history has been celebrated by the drinking of quite so many toasts as the winning of the War for Independence. When Congress demobilized the Continental Army, Washington's triumphal journey into retirement was the occasion for a series of banquets at which the formal toasts numbered a symbolic thirteen. At Annapolis Washington added a fourteenth: "Sufficient Powers to Congress for general purposes!" And when he took leave of his officers at Fraunces Tavern in New York he "filled a wine glass" and offered the most widely quoted toast of his career: "With a heart full of love and gratitude, I now take leave of you. I most devoutly wish that your latter days may be as prosperous and happy as your former ones have been glorious and honorable."

While Washington was being toasted as "the Man who Unites all Hearts" and "Columbia's Favorite Son," the members of a convivial London health club, called "The Anacreontic Society," were meeting at the Crown and Anchor Tavern, where they opened their meetings with raised glasses and the singing of their club song, "To Anacreon in Heaven." The anthem, which toasted the memory of the Greek poet who had declared life to be an eternal round of healths, concluded:

While thus we agree,
Our toast let it be,
May our club flourish happy, united, and free!
And long may the sons of Anacreon entwine
The myrtle of Venus with Bacchus' Vine!

The melody, which every American would immediately recognize as that of "The Star-Spangled Banner," was first adapted to Yankee use as a tribute to "Adams and Liberty" and was later used as the musical setting for the stirring stanzas written by Francis Scott Key.

Another old eighteenth-century toasting song, "Auld Lang Syne," was fated to become the midnight anthem of all English-speaking New Year's Eve celebrants. The melody was supposed to have been borrowed from the music of the Roman Catholic Church and the words copied down by Robert Burns from the lips of an old Scottish singer. In the land of lively jigs and brimming jiggers, the mood of boozy nostalgia was not confined to one night of the year, however. Clannish quaffers were prepared to share "a cup of kindness" at any season and have traditionally saluted each other with practical wishes for "Mair sense and mair silver!" and "Health, wealth, wit and meal!"—and with that most canny of all alcoholic benedictions, "Lang may your lum reek [or "Long may your chimney smoke"] wi' ither folks' coal!" But, in justice to the Scots, a similar emphasis upon material well-being is to be found in other folk toasts as well, from the Irish Gaelic *Sheed Arth!* ("May you always wear silk!") to the Spanish *¡Salud, pesetas y amor!* ("Health, money and love!").

In the opinion of the Reverend Richard Valpy French, rector of Llanmartin and Wilcrick, who gave a temperance lecture that was published in 1880 as the first and only history of toasting in the English language, the drinking of healths, "especially in Scotch society, was tyrannically enforced." In the early 1800's persons named in a toast were bound to acknowledge the honor "by placing the right hand on the heart, saying in a very distinct and audible voice, and with a smile of gratification on the countenance, 'Your good health,' then drinking off the glass of wine." At any well-run dinner party, the host was obliged to "drink the health of every one of the guests, who were obliged to follow suit, so that supposing ten people to be present, no less than ninety healths would be drunk. The ladies participated in this part of the entertainment, and before they retired they had to take part in another species of drinking diversion, *i.e.* the *rounds of toasts.* This little game was played thus —each lady present had to name an absent gentleman, and each gentleman an absent lady . . . and the pair being thus matched, were toasted together amidst many jocular allusions to the fitness of the union." Of all such guzzling games, the Reverend French singles out the drinking of "sentiments" as the one which "filled Lord Cockburn with the greatest disgust." This was a kind of round robin in which each person was asked to contribute some pretty little platitude to which all could drink. Among the many "idiotic inanities" calculated to make Lord Cockburn queasy with revulsion were such genteel gems as "May the pleasures of the evening bear the reflections of the morning. . . . May the hand of charity wipe away the tear from the eye of sorrow. . . . May the wings of friendship never molt a feather." It was "a most tyrannical custom," the Reverend French concludes, "to which everybody was compelled to conform."

Unlike Lord Cockburn and the abstemious Rector of Wilcrick, most Scots and Englishmen were quite amiably disposed to drink to any sentiment that did not dishonor their country's flag or cast doubt upon their mothers' virtue:

"Oaken ships, and British hands to man them!"

"Merry hearts to village maidens!"

"May the game laws be repealed!"

"May the village 'belle' never be too long in the clapper!"

"May the skin of your bum never cover a drum!"

"Lots of beef, oceans of beer, a pretty girl and a thousand a year!"

The last toast, with its heroic allusion to "oceans of beer," presumably dates from the passage of the Beer Bill of 1832, when legislation was introduced to induce the British workingman to kick the gin habit in favor of milder malt beverages. In the interest of national temperance, 30,000 beer shops were opened within a year and Britons responded to the challenge by drinking more beer and gin, too. "Everybody is drunk," Sydney Smith reported. "Those who are not singing are sprawling. The sovereign people are in a beastly state."

When young Victoria inherited the throne in 1837, her swacked and sprawling subjects enthusiastically toasted "The Queen, God bless her!" By 1845, a fad for adding shouts of "huzza" to every toast had become standard procedure. "Nine times nine cheers" were given for " 'Er royal Majesty" and any deserving 'Arry, 'Erbert or Halbert—a noisy ritual that eventually diminished into a restrained twentieth-century murmur of "Cheers."

With or without huzzas, the practice of toasting had to be abolished, temperance forces were still insisting a generation later. "Would that the archbishops and bishops of the Church of England would cease to submit to these appendages at public breakfasts, luncheons and dinners," the Reverend French exclaimed from his temperance platform in 1880, and cited, by way of example, a newspaper account of an "educational dinner" at which " 'The Royal Family' was drunk; 'Her Majesty's

Ministers' were drunk; 'The Houses of Parliament' were drunk; 'The Universities of Scotland' were drunk; 'Popular Education in its extended sense' was drunk; 'The Clergy of Scotland of all Denominations' were drunk; 'The Parish Schoolmasters' were drunk; other parties not named were drunk; 'The Fine Arts' were drunk; 'The Press' was drunk . . ."

An equally healthful state of affairs had long obtained in democratic America, where, for more than a century, "The President of the United States" was drunk; "The Members of both Houses of Congress" were drunk; "The American Farmer" and "The American Eagle" were drunk; "The Wives and Mothers of all Free Men" were drunk—together with the governors, legislators, citizens and judiciary of all the several sovereign states. "Drink rum, drink rum, drink rum, by gum, with me," expressed the will of a free and thirsty people whose manifest destiny can be traced through the innumerable slogans and rallying cries which have served Americans as an excuse for a glass, a mug or a gallon jug: "Tippecanoe and Tyler too!" "Fifty-four Forty or Fight!" "Remember the Alamo!" "Pike's Peak or Bust!" "The Union Forever!" "The Stars and the Bars!" "Remember the Maine!" "To hell with the Kaiser!" "Happy days are here again!" "Remember Pearl Harbor!" "Keep 'em flying!" "Get America moving again!"

In the days of "wooden ships and iron men," official toasts were in the patriotic vein of naval hero Stephen Decatur's "Our country: in her intercourse with foreign nations may she always be right; but our country, right or wrong!" But in grog shops along the water front the old bosun's toast was more likely to be this:

Here's to the ships of our Navy,
And the ladies of our land,
May the first be ever well rigged,
And the latter ever well manned!

While a gentleman of the old South might propose a courtly toast "To the ladies, God bless them," the Irish immigrant of the North was likely to be knocking back a crock of "blue ruin" with "Here's to the flea that jumped over me and bit the behind of me missus!" While literary and social lights of New York and Boston were toasting the delights of sherry with verses from Omar Khayyám, earthy Pennsylvania Dutchmen set the scene for a shot of schnapps with this:

So drink ich, so stink ich,
Drink ich net, so stink ich doch,
So ist besser gedrinka und gestunka
Os net gedrunka, und doch gestunka!

Which may be translated as, "If I drink, I stink. If I don't drink, I stink anyway. So it's better to drink and stink than to *not* drink and stink anyway!" Though the jargon was mostly German, the reasoning was 100-proof American. In the great age of folk toasting that preceded Prohibition, Americans drank to just about every sentiment conceivable and in a wide range of moods. Some toasts were a strange blend of friendliness and hostility:

Here's a toast for you and me:
And may we never disagree;
But if we do, then to hell with you.
So here's to me!

Some expressed a touching fondness for a few close friends and cherished possessions:

Hail, good old hat, my companion devoted!
Hail, good old shoes, blest deliverers from pain!
Hail, good old glass, my unfailing inspirer!
Hail, good old friends, ne'er appealed to in vain!

Others were frankly Oedipal:

Here's to the happiest days of my life,
Spent in the arms of another man's wife
—My mother!

Some were dependent rather than devoted and raised the thorny question, "Is there booze after death?":

Here's to you and you and you!
If I should die and go to Heaven, and not find you,
I would turn around and go to hell,
Just to be with you and you and you!

Others were defiantly fatalistic:

Here's to hell! May the stay there
Be as much fun as the way there!

There were toasts for tightwads:

Lift 'em high and drain 'em dry
To the guy who says, "My turn to buy!"

There were toasts for truculent underachievers:

Here's to the men who lose!
It is the vanquished's praises that I sing,
And this is the toast I choose:
"A hard-fought failure is a noble thing!"

And there was even a short production number for whimsical nature lovers:

A wee little dog passed a wee little tree.
Said the wee little tree, "Won't you have one on me?"
"No," said the little dog, no bigger than a mouse.
"I just had one on the house."

But the favorite toast was still a woman. To her face, the ladies' man of the eighties and nineties might raise his glass and murmur, "I have known many, liked a few, loved but one, darling—here's to you!" But in the all-male atmosphere of the corner saloon the same smooth-toasting Lothario could earn comradely guffaws and envious glances with this:

Here's to you, and here's to me,
Here's to the girl with the dimpled knee.
Here's to the boy who fastened her garter;
It wasn't much—but a darned good starter!

Another swain, either less fortunate or more truthful, might be moved to declaim sadly:

Here's to dear Alice, so sweet and good.
God made Alice—I wish I *could!*

Which, in turn, might inspire a recitation of this:

Here's to the girl who lives on the hill.
She won't, but her sister will.
So here's to her sister!

In the opinion of one temperance poet of the early twentieth century, anybody's sister would, if she were properly plied with passionate toasts. "Oh, lovely maids!" he expostulated:

Never for all Pactolus' wealth,
In wine let lover drink your health!
Beware the traitor who shall dare
For you the cursed draught prepare . . .

As the tempo of American drinking began to swing from a wine-and-beery waltz time to a jazzy cocktail quickstep, male toasters contributed to the growing emancipation of women by concocting draughts that would liberate even the most fettered female libido and boy-girl toasts became more outspoken. Removing the rakish overseas cap which was part of his World War I uniform, the citizen-soldier toasted his sweetheart of the week with a peppy switch on a sentiment that had once made Lord Cockburn limp with nausea:

Here's to the wings of love—
May they never molt a feather,
Till my big boots and your little shoes
Are under the bed together!

While even the most emancipated American girl might blush or giggle at the directness of this approach, doughboys found that French *mesdemoiselles* were likely to seize the amorous initiative with the following candid couplet:

Je vous baissez, je vous amour.
Si voulez-vous, je vous encore.

Which few members of the Signal Corps needed to have decoded as, "I kiss you, I love you. If you wish, I'll do it again." The French toast, Yanks soon learned, was not only *A votre sante!* or "To your health!" but *A vos amours!*—"To your loves!"—with a regard for the plural that brought French grammar into complete agreement with the facts of French life. "Here's to the girl who gives and forgives and never sells!" a Gallic grenadier would thunder with the aid of English subtitles. "Here's to the man who gets and forgets and never tells!" "*A nos femmes, à nos chevaux et à ceux qui les montent!*" the cavalryman could be heard to reply: "To our women, our horses and the men who ride them!"

Italian infantrymen toasted and trudged to the tune

of "*Viva, viva, viva l'amor . . . viva la compagnia!*" British Tommies of the Middlesex Regiment drank "Here's to the Middlesex! Here's to the fair sex! Here's to the middle of the fair sex!" Battalions who fought their way through Flanders found the friendly Flemings eager to drink "*Dat we het nog lang mogen mogen!*" "That we may still like it for a long time!" And troops who went the whole route into Germany found that *Prosit!* was prosaic compared to the boy-girl *Brüderschaft* toast, in which everlasting "brotherhood" was drunk by linking one's drinking arm through that of a frolicsome *Fräulein* for a face-to-face rendition:

Trink, trink, Brüderlein, trink;
Geh' nicht alleine nach Haus!
Meide den Kummer und meide den Schmerz,
Dann ist das Leben ein Scherz!

This was followed by a most unbrotherly kiss and repeated until both parties were higher than a *Gemütlichkeit:* "Drink, drink, brother dear, drink; do not go home alone! Avoid sorrow and pain, and all your life will be fun."

Willst du Bier, Komm zu mir!—"If you want beer, you must come here!"—was not the slogan of the American Anti-Saloon League, however. A parched and troublesome future lay in store for the States even as home-front wags hoisted their glasses in joking tribute to the ax-wielding, bar-smashing lady leader of the militant "Drys":

Here's to Carry Nation,
Of antidrink renown,
Who, though against libation,
Hit ev'ry bar in town!

When American veterans returned home, they barely had time to say "Here's mud in your eye!" before Prohibition was upon them and American toasting was on its way to becoming a lost art. Raw bootleg booze and the quick-shot speak-easy atmosphere did not lend themselves to the savoring of either sauce or sentiment:

I'm tired of drinking toasts for each little shot of gin,
Let's toss out all the hooey, and toss the alky in!

Such were the jingled but unpoetic views of most speak-easy patrons, whose desire for the forbidden delights of alcohol often exceeded that for the pleasures of the boudoir:

When I want it, I want it awful bad.
When I don't get it, it makes me awful mad.
When I do get it, it makes me, oh, so frisky—
Don't get me wrong, I mean a shot of whisky!

Though naughty women were much more available than good Scotch, sex was not entirely overlooked. But the excuse for a fast blast of hooch was less likely to be a woman than it was the act of intercourse itself:

Here's to it, and to it again!
If you get to it and don't do it,
You may never get to it to do it again!

The Jazz Age, in which so many matrons and grandmothers bobbed their hair, rolled their hose and tried to pass as giddy young flappers, led to this mock solemnity:

Here's to the man who takes a wife,
Let him make no mistake:
For it makes a world of difference
Whose wife it is you take!

Talk of eugenics, free love and contraception was responsible for a spate of gag toasts, such as this one:

Here's to the bee, that busy soul;
He has no time for birth control.
That's why it is, in times like these,
We have so many sons of bees!

Prohibition was still in full force when a fad for things collegiate put drinkers of all ages into raccoon coats and hip-flaskers who had flunked out of high school lifted their steins and highball glasses "to dear old Maine" at the soulfully crooned behest of an Ivy-League-type bandleader named Rudy Vallee. The University of Maine became the alcoholic alma mater of the masses and the classes, along with such great toasting institutions as Georgia Tech, whose famous "Rambling wreck" song gave rah-rah encouragement to thousands of unmatriculated rummies:

I'd drink to ev'ry fellow who comes from far and near;
I'm a rambling wreck from Georgia Tech and a hell of an engineer!

Since Joe College was also likely to be one hell of a drinker, fraternity brothers made a ritual of singing—until Joe had drained his glass, stein or pitcher—"Here's to Joe, he's true blue. He's a drunkard, through and through! Drink it down, chug-a-lug, chug-a-lug." On the eve of the 1929 stock-market crash, affluent frosh were offering humorous healths "To dad—the kin you love to touch!" But with the onset of the Depression, unemployed alumni and undergraduates on short allowances were seldom in the mood for anything more spirited than "Here's how" or "Down the hatch." Repeal of the Eighteenth Amendment brought back legal beer and bonded whisky, but no event in the past thirty years has managed to inspire a renaissance in American toasting. Except at weddings and formal banquets, it would seem that American toasting has been reduced to a mumbled repetition of "Cheers," "Skoal" and "Prosit," with an occasional "Bottoms up" or "Here's to it."

A similar decline in toasting is said to have taken place in Japan, where ornate feudal healths have been streamlined down into something that sounds like "Can pay!" and suave sake sippers salute each other with sentiments like "I think you are getting along very well!" and "You seem to have put on weight, haven't you?"

Translated to these shores, such highly provocative healths could only lead to misunderstandings and hasten a return to Prohibition. In a fluid society, such as our own, the interested health enthusiast would do better to experiment with toasts to blondes, brunettes, redheads, Republicans, Democrats, repeal of the income-tax laws, planned parenthood for Belgian rabbits—or anything else that strikes his fancy. But it would seem likely that mass enthusiasm for toasting could be aroused most easily by drinking to the joys of drinking itself. Other cultures have long since recognized that booze is, after all, the best excuse for a glass that man has ever devised. Hence, the Russians have traditionally promoted peaceful coexistence among themselves with "Drink until green imps appear!" and the Germans with "Drink until your nose shines red as a carbuncle, that it may be your light in this life's darkness!"

"Hurray for enjoyment, hurray for fun! We're going home drunk!" is a year-round Portuguese toast which most Americans would openly endorse only at Yuletide—the one season of the year when we abandon our usual mumbled monosyllables for the exuberant eloquence of "Merry Christmas!" and "Happy New Year!" Though unsuitable for use in August and inappropriate for weddings and *bar mizvahs*, "Merry Christmas" and "Happy New Year" are undoubtedly the two jolliest toasts we have and can hold their own with such exotic seasonal toasts as the French *Joyeux Noel!*, the Spanish *¡Feliz Navidad!* and the Italian *Buone Natale!*

Depending on where one spends the holidays, the Christmas toast may be *Gledelig Jul!* (Norwegian),

Vroolijk Kerfeest! (Dutch), *Weselych Swiat!* (Polish) or *Mele Kalikimaka!* (Hawaiian). But regardless of where one winds up on New Year's Eve, some fuddled fellow is bound to clap his hand on your shoulder and address you as follows:

Oes o lwydd gwir sylweddol—a gaffo
'N deg effaith hanfodol—
A Gwynfa 'n ei ran, ar ol,
Yn gu haddef dragwyddol!

He could be relating a risqué rhyme about a swell li'l doll named Gwynfa. Or he might be inquiring if you are the owner of the blue Chevy that's parked in the driveway with no air in the tires. But if he happens to be a Welshman, he's actually reciting a toast to your earthly success and offering the wish that Paradise may be your everlasting home.

Those who are not conversant in Welsh may make a reasonably appropriate reply by repeating the Albanian for "May you be happy too!": *Gëzuar gofsh!*

Should he counter with "*Brromp!*," don't put him down for "Swine drunke." It only means that he's challenging you to a friendly drink in your adopted tongue.

Clink your glass against his with a smart *twange*, bow three times, kisse your fingers, and reply with a resonant "*Brromp pach!*" "I accept your challenge!"

V

SWEARING

Swearing

The custom of offering verbal felicities in the form of a toast has been closely allied to the ancient practice of swearing since shortly after the Flood, when a half-fuddled old wine fancier named Noah roused himself to exclaim, "Cursed be Canaan . . . Blessed be the Lord God of Shem."

Theory has it that the earliest form of antediluvian "swearing" was largely a matter of growls, hisses and roars calculated to strike fear in the ear of an enemy. As Finley Peter Dunne once put it, in the dialect of Mr. Dooley, " 'Twas intinded as a compromise between runnin' away an' fightin'. Befure it was invinted they was on'y th' two ways out iv an argymint."

This view is both extremely primitive and extremely modern. It takes into account the familiar business of swearing *at* but ignores the age-old ritual of oath-taking —of swearing *by* (God, Zeus, the Beard of the Prophet, etc.) and swearing *on* (the Bible, the Koran or some sacred relic or object). And it is from swearing solemn oaths that we evolved the basic language for aggressive-type swearing: the verbal irreverence toward things sacred and taboo that we call "profanity."

Like prayer, profanity has its roots in primitive religion. Granted the gift of speech, Man turned out to be a born liar, and truth was attested to by pledges made in the names of pagan nature gods and superhuman forces. Norsemen swore by Thor and Frigga. Early Goths swore by thunder and lightning, and ancient Arabs swore by all the mysterious laxative powers of the fig.

Regardless of such potent guarantees, many oaths were sworn falsely, however. A guilty Slovenian tribesman would lay his hand upon the Holy Oak and protest his innocence with the words "May Perkun destroy me!" And if Perkun did not destroy him, the shifty knave soon began swearing by Perkun whenever he jolly well felt like it—fearlessly and profanely—until Perkun's power was discredited and the religion passed away.

It was this sort of irreverence that the Hebrews refused to tolerate on behalf of Jehovah. The Third Commandment was directed specifically against such "vain" swearing, and Levitical punishment for the blasphemous use of God's name was death. Similar strictures were placed upon curses or prayers that evil might befall others—though circumstances seemed to alter cases and the Bible remains a handbook of hair-raising maledictions.

Throughout the rest of the ancient world, where the names of deities were not so well protected, truth was pledged by an ever-increasing variety of oaths. Egyptians, who once swore by Isis and Osiris, began to swear by the mystic qualities of the onion, the garlic and the leek. Greeks, who swore by all the gods, invoked the names of the goose, the caper, the dog, and the Rhodesian cabbage—a vegetable venerated as a heaven-sent hang-over cure. But as the names of animals, vegetables and divinities became debased through misuse, profanity flourished and the Greek-on-the-street would grumble "Great Zeus!" or "By the cabbage!" at every Athenian annoyance. Restrictions applied only to Hercules' name, which was reserved for the use of children, who were free to swear with it out of doors but were punished for using it in the house.

For some unknown reason, the playtime profanity of Greek kiddies later became the exclusive expletive of Roman men, in the form of *Mehercule!* Roman women, not to be outdone in any kind of profligacy, swore profanely by Castor, and *Mecastor!* became a feminine oath. Latin sexual slang, on the other hand, was used freely by both men and women and was not considered profanity at all. Names and epithets suggestive of bawdry, nymphomania, bastardy and perversion were familiar terms of endearment and figured mainly in friendly banter.

Julius, a swearing Caesar, who had earned every sexual laurel known to street language, rejoiced in the soldiers' marching song that hailed his triumphant return from Gaul:

Home we bring our bald whoremonger;
Romans, lock your wives away!
All the bags of gold you lent him
Went his Gallic tarts to pay.

Among the many legal terms deriving from Latin are "jury" and "perjury," both of which originate in *jurare* ("to swear," in the formal, legalistic sense). Such oath-taking among Romans reflected the man-worship of a powerful state religion, and the most solemn oath was taken on the head of the living emperor. Caligula, who erected a shrine to himself, where peacocks and flamingos were sacrificed to his golden image, preferred to have the populace swear by his divine Genius. His own most binding oaths were sworn by the name of his sister Drusilla, one of three with whom he regularly indulged in incestuous intimacies while lying down to dinner in the presence of his wife and guests.

While Caligula's peculiar table manners were occasioning murmurs of "By Jove!" and "Ye gods!" in the original Latin, the deep-freeze warriors of the North were pledging alliances by the power of the sword. It was not until centuries later, when Europe was Christianized, that God was called upon to witness oaths made by the naked blade and the sword became a symbol of the Holy Cross.

With Frankish fervor, Charlemagne demanded that allegiance be sworn *Sic me adjuvet Deus*, "So help me God," the oath still used in our present-day courts. The Latin name for God, *Deus*, is profanely echoed in our own word "deuce"—generally considered a euphemism for "damn." The notion that "deuce" was borrowed from the ancient game of dice is given support by most dictionaries, where the origins of "deuce" are traced to *duos*, the Latin word for "two." The implication is that *duos* was the Roman equivalent of "snake eyes" and hence an expression of anger. Unfortunately for the theory, however, Caesar's sportsmen rolled four bones instead of two and crapped out on a show of four one-spots. This was known as *canicula*, or "little dog," and gave birth to a litter of quite different expressions based on *Damnosa canicula!* ("Damned little dog!")

As Christianity spread, the names of saints, shrines and sacred relics were used as guarantees of truthtelling and soon found their way into profanity's growing word list. Men swore "by God's wounds," "by God's blood" and by "the bell of the abbey church." In an effort to combat the rising flood of impious swearing, Charlemagne made it punishable under law, but penalties were not nearly so severe as under Kenneth II, king of Scots, who chastised tenth-century offenders by cutting out their tongues. France's Philip II disposed of the problem by drowning swearers in the Seine, while Louis IX set a precedent for the traditional soap-in-mouth treatment by branding their tongues with a hot iron.

The sainted Louis' pet peeve was the courtly habit of blithely swearing *pardieu!* (by God!), *cordieu!* (God's heart!) and *tetedieu!* (God's head!). Luckily, Louis also had a pet dog named Bleu, and courtiers who had no taste for hot irons were able to swear their way around the law by substituting the dog's name for the name of the Deity—*parbleu, corbleu!, sacre bleu!* and so forth, in the manner familiar to Frenchmen ever since.

The practice of swearing by God's head, heart, blood and wounds resulted from the preachments of the medieval clergy upon the detailed agonies of the Crucifixion and eventually came to include God's liver, eyelids, feet, toes and nails. The nails of the Cross were known as "God's hooks" and in time became the jocular "Gadzooks!" or "Zooks!" In like fashion we have "'Sblood" for "God's blood," "'Sdeath" for "God's death" and "'Swounds" for "God's wounds"—the last being variously rendered as "Zwounds!" or "Zounds!" or "Zoonds!" "Odds bodkins!"—which any twentieth-century child may use indoors or out—originally referred to God's body in the blasphemously diminutive form of "bodikins" and is literally "God's little body!"

On the whole, English monarchs were far more tolerant of such swearing than were their Continental counterparts. Richard the Lion-Hearted swore "by God's legs" and his brother John swore "by God's teeth." And when Henry I set a scale of penalties for blasphemy, nobles, squires and yeomen were fined in shillings, with only the lowly pages sentenced "to be whipt."

The prevalence and casualness of English religious profanity are evident from Chaucer's tales of the Canterbury pilgrims, whose speech was spiced with such impious interjections as "By goddes corpus," "for goddes herte," and "by seint Ronyon!" Mildest of all were the oaths of Sir Thopas, who swore "by ale and bread," and the Prioress, whose "grettest oath was but by St. Eloy." Most numerous and various were the oaths of "Our Hoste," who "lough and swoor" at the least provocation:

" 'Ye,' quod our hoste, 'by Seint Poules belle.' "

" 'Harrow!' quod he, 'by nayles and by blood!' "

That such profanity was common to all Europe is apparent from the exclamations Rabelais uses to describe the public panic during the urinary flood unleashed by the giant Gargantua:

" '*Pocapedion!* God's head!' roared a Gascon.

" '*Das dich Gots leyden Schend!*' bellowed a German trooper. 'God's passion roil you!'

" '*Pote de Christo!*' an Italian voice rang out. 'Christ's power!'

" '*Ventre St. Quenet!* . . . By the bellies of all the apostles . . . God's virtue . . . by St. Fiacre of the land of Brie!' "

In order to enjoy the comforts of swearing without incurring the penalties of profanity, the French invented a calendar of fictitious saints' names to swear with—St. Lâche, the patron of idlers; St. Nitouche, who watched over hypocrites; and St. Gris, beloved of drunkards—to which the ribald Rabelais adds a medley of his own: "By St. Godegran, stoned to death with apple dumplings . . . by St. Foutin, the fornicator's friend! . . . by St. Vitus and his jig! . . . by Ste. Mamica, the virgin martyr, by our lusty mammical duty to all virgins!"

To avoid profaning the Holy Name, the English

began to swear "by the cross of the mousefoot" and made changes in the spelling and pronunciation of "by God" that seem even more blasphemous: "I'cod," "by Gog" and "by Cock and pye." In *London Lyckpenny*, the oldest English street ballad, "pye" was dropped from the last phrase and the oath was abbreviated to a breezy "Yea, by Cock!"

It was in the same fifteenth century that "goddamn" was first heard, bursting from the lips of British soldiers sent to fight in France. So common was this military oath that the French adopted it as a nickname for all Englishmen. When the child monarch, Henry VI, assumed the thrones of England and France, he was known as "Little King Goddamn." British profanity persisted, and the name stuck. Three centuries later, English officers in Paris were hailed with "Here come the goddamns!" and the traveler in Portugal was greeted with a friendly, "How do you do, Jack? Damn you!"

The more specific "goddamn it" and "goddamn you" didn't come into use until the close of the sixteenth century. "God damn me" appears as a new phrase in Shakespeare's *Comedy of Errors*, where it is described as common to the speech of low women: " 'God damn me;' that's as much to say, 'God make me a light wench.' "

Though Shakespeare's queen, Elizabeth, angrily swore "By God's Son!" and "God's death!" the Bard's ladies were generally given to more genteel expressions—as witness Hotspur's comment upon the mildness of Lady Percy's "in good sooth" in the first part of *Henry IV:* "Heart! you swear like a comfit-maker's wife. . . . Swear me, Kate, like a lady as thou art, a good mouth-filling oath . . ."

No age was more class-conscious in its swearing, and an easy command of vigorous expressions was a sure sign of Elizabethan status. In Ben Jonson's *Every Man in His Humor*, Master Stephen, a country bumpkin, listens in awe as the swaggering Captain Bobadil thunders, "A whoreson filthy slave, a dung-worm, an excrement! Body o' Caesar, but that I seem to let forth so mean a spirit, I'd have stabb'd him to the earth. . . . By Pharaoh's foot, I would have done it!"

"Oh, he swears most admirably," the status-seeking Stephen murmurs. "By Pharaoh's foot! Body o' Caesar! — I shall never do it, sure. Upon mine honor, and by St. George! — No, I have not the right grace."

"He that swereth depe, swereth like a lorde," Thomas Elyot had observed—and a cursory survey of Shakespeare's plays reveals that his noblemen were indeed inspired in their use of munchy-crunchy invective. "Bloody, bawdy villain!" Hamlet rants at the peak of princely passion. "Remorseless, treacherous, lecherous, kindless villain!" And when Prince Hal berates Falstaff as "this sanguine coward, this bed-presser, this horseback-breaker, this hill of flesh," the noble Sir John replies with a barrage of fine phallic scurrilities: " 'Sblood, you starveling, you elf-skin, you dried neat's tongue, you bull's pizzle, you stock-fish! O for breath to utter what is like thee! you tailor's-yard, you sheath, you bow-case, you vile standing tuck!"

"Swear horrible," Sir Toby Belch advised Sir Andrew Aguecheek; and if profanity began to assume a new sexual emphasis, the cause may be laid to the new secular spirit that arose with the Reformation. In *The Shoemaker's Holiday*, the workhorse of modern sexual profanity made a coltish stage entrance in a wordplay upon the name of the journeyman Firk. The shoemaker, who addresses his wife as "hopperarse" and "Dame Clapperdudgeon," shouts in a moment of critical stress, "Peace, you bombast-cotton-candle-queen . . . quarrel not with me and my men; with me and my fine Firk; I'll firk you, if you do!"

The suggested word, which entered English by way of the Anglo-Saxon *fachan*, meaning "to take or seize," appears in Shakespeare's *The Merry Wives of Windsor* in the guise of "focative," when Sir Hugh Evans asks, "What's the focative case, William?" Eric Partridge, who has compiled a scholarly glossary of the Swan of Avon's numerous sexual flights, adds the note that "*F**k*" is probably one of the sadistic group of words for the man's part in copulation (cf. *clap*, *cope*, *hit*, *strike*, *thump*, and the modern slang term, *bang*), for it seems to derive from the German *ficken*, 'to strike,' as Klüge maintains. Probably confirmatory rather than contradictory is Sanskrit *ukshan* (a bull; literally, impregnator), which Bopp, in his *Comparative Grammar*, maintains to have originally been *fukshan*. . ." In *Origins*, his etymological dictionary, Partridge states that "*F**k* shares with *c**t* two distinctions: they are the only two Standard English words excluded from all general and etymological dictionaries since the eighteenth century and the only two Standard English words that, outside of medical or semi-official reports and learned papers, still cannot be printed in full anywhere within the British Commonwealth."

The much-heralded British court clearance of *Lady*

Chatterley's Lover has changed the situation since Partridge wrote the above in 1950, however. Citizens of the Commonwealth are now free to enjoy the unexpurgated experience of seeing both words spelled out in all four letters, together with such sweet nothings as *p**s* and *s**t.* Considered only vaguely vulgar by Elizabethan standards, *p**s* was employed by Shakespeare as a noun in *The Tempest,* a verb in *The Merry Wives of Windsor* and an adjectival synonym for "brief" ("a pissing while") in *Two Gentlemen of Verona.* The old five-letter word "shyte," which belongs to the same family as "sheet" and "shoot," appeared in *The Metamorphosis of Ajax,* the book in which Elizabeth's ribald-rhyming godson, Sir John Harington, published his plans for the flush toilet.

In this period of emerging sexual profanity, clerical censure was still directed against the old 'Sblood and Zounds. A plan put before Lord Burghley estimated that by levying fines against such swearing England could increase her annual income by 20,000,000 crowns, but Elizabeth was too partial to the habit herself to favor such a measure. Puritan agitation was strong, however, and two years after Elizabeth's death Parliament passed an act imposing a ten-pound penalty upon the use of profanity in a theatrical performance. This was a staggering sum at a time when eight pounds was the most a playwright could hope to make on a new play, and the law had the effect of inhibiting writers to the point where Elizabethan gusto vanished from the stage.

Cheered by success, antiprofanity forces then managed to push through a statute imposing a fine of twelve-pence on all swearers, and those who could not pay were sent to the stocks. A public agency was established to enforce the law, and parish deputies were appointed to collect fines on a commission basis, with the result that citizens of Chittlehampton were held guilty for saying "Upon my life!" Puritan punishment in Cromwell's army was so extreme that one Boutholmey, a quartermaster charged with profanity, was sentenced "to have his tongue bored with a red-hot iron, his sword broken over his head, and himself ignominiously dismissed from the service."

Despite all laws and penalties, people continued to swear throughout the dour days of the Commonwealth. Following the Restoration, milady's expletives and milord's ejaculations were, for the most part, gay revivals of Zooks and Damn. "God" had become "Odd," as in "Odds body" or "Odsbud," and "Lord" became "Lud" or "La!" Clandestine amours were rampant, cuckoldry was in flower and sexual name-calling was a social grace. A short sampler of His and Her stage swearing illustrates the period style:

"A Pox o' this Impertinent Lady Fancyfull, and her Plots, and her French-woman too. She's a Whimsical Ill natur'd Bitch."

"Oh la, Sir, you'll make me asham'd."

"Damned senseless, impudent virtuous jade!"

"My Father calls, you plaguey devil."

"Ah Hussy! Hussy! — Come home, you Slut!"

"Zooks! 'tis the captain!"

"Beasts, Jades, Jilts, Harpies, Furies, Whores!"

"O lud! he has almost cracked my head."

"Zounds, sirrah!"

" 'Sdeath and hell!"

Selected from ten different plays, the above dialogue might serve as an actual scene in any comedy of the sexes written during the century between Wycherley and Goldsmith. Of all words, only "pox" need be explained, since it referred to neither the chicken- nor the small-varieties but was the name given to syphilis at a time when such ailments were "social" in every sense of the word.

The apogee of eighteenth-century oddity was reached with the "oath referential" used by Bob Acres in Sheridan's *The Rivals*. The idea here was to adapt one's swearing to each change of subject. If the talk was of coach travel, the oath was "Odds whips and wheels!" Mention of honor called for "Odds crowns and laurels!" while matters military were greeted with "Odds triggers and flints!" and "Odds balls and barrels!"

"Ha! ha! 'tis genteel, isn't it!" Bob Acres exclaims.

"Very genteel, and very new, indeed!" Captain Absolute agrees. "And I dare say will supplant all other figures of imprecation."

"Ay, ay, the best terms will grow obsolete. — Damns have had their day."

Happily, for the sanity of the English, the prophecy was not borne out. "Damn" and "goddamn" continued in the repertoire of lords, lackeys and the famed Billingsgate fishwives, whose versatile invective made "billingsgate" a synonym for swearing. A statute against swearing still remained on the books, and antiprofanity groups pressed for its enforcement against all classes. In 1718 a

London journalist named Burridge was tried for blasphemy and ordered "to take up a position at the New Church in the Strand and to be from there publicly whipped to Charing Cross"—after which he was fined and given a month in jail.

The ever-present possibility of ruffling the lunatic fringe led the Reverend Laurence Sterne, author of *Tristram Shandy*, to indicate even the commonly used "arse" with asterisks. Commenting on the use of dots and dashes, the cheerful churchman wittily observed: "Take the dash away, and write Backside, —'tis Bawdy. Scratch Backside out, and put Covered-way in, 'tis a Metaphor."

In the matter of profanity, Sterne's views were undoubtedly at one with those of his hero's father, Mr. Shandy, who believed that small curses upon great occasions "are but so much waste of our strength." In order to have a selection of large curses for all occasions, Shandy, Sr., kept handy a copy of an actual form of excommunication composed by the Bishop Ernulphus, in which a thesaurus of maledictions was compounded in the names of the saints, the angels and every conceivable Holy Personage:

" '. . . May he be cursed in eating and drinking, in being hungry, in being thirsty, in fasting, in sleeping, in slumbering, in walking, in standing, in sitting, in lying, in working, in resting, in pissing, in shitting, and in bloodletting!' "

" 'May he be cursed in his reins, and in his groin,' (God in heaven forbid! quoth my Uncle Toby) 'in his thighs, in his genitals,' (my father shook his head) 'and in his hips, and in his knees, his legs, and feet, and toe-nails!' "

The cumulative force of the anathema, which runs to four pages, prompts the bemused Uncle Toby to remark, "Our armies swore terribly in Flanders." To which an equally bemused nephew of Uncle Sam can only add, "So did our American army during the Revolutionary War." Indeed, Yankee oaths were so numerous and pungent that General George Washington was obliged to issue a personal communiqué on the subject in 1779:

"Many and pointed orders have been issued against that unmeaning and abominable custom of swearing, notwithstanding which, with much regret, the General observes that it prevails, if possible, more than ever . . . For the sake, therefore, of religion, decency, and order, the General hopes and trusts that the officers of every rank will use their influence and authority to check a vice which is as unprofitable as it is wicked and shameful."

In an earlier order issued by John Adams, naval officers were authorized to punish swearing sailors "by causing them to wear a wooden collar or some shameful badge," but such orders were generally ignored by American officers trained in the great British tradition of "damn" and "hell." Washington's own conversation was reputed to be amply spiced with both of these gentlemanly oaths, though he seldom indulged in the hard profanity used in patriot ranks. According to the earwitness account of General Charles Scott, however, Washington swore one day at Monmouth "until the leaves shook on the trees. Charming, delightful! Never have I enjoyed such swearing before or since. Sir, on that day, he swore like an angel from heaven."

Unfortunately, no one had the foresight to jot down Washington's historic words. But there is some reassurance in the knowledge that the Father of Our Country was capable of virtuoso performance in an American art that began with the early settlers—for all the Pilgrims were not Puritans and a small band of devoted swearers succeeded in planting the seeds of profanity in the New World against all odds and Blue Laws. By 1699 an English visitor was able to report that, despite their sanctity, the northern colonists were "very prophane in their common dialect." The Reverend Jonathan Boucher, traveling in Maryland at a still later date, complained of the constant use of "obscene conceits and broad expressions," and the British Captain Thomas Morris duly recorded that during an Indian raid, "One of the Delaware nation . . . passing by the cabin where I lay, called out in broken English: 'Damned son of a bitch!' "

The phrase used by this disgruntled Delaware was the last great classical invention in Anglo-American swearing. Dating from 1712, it was contrived as a euphemism for the earlier "whoreson," or "son of a whore," and represented a continuing trend toward verbal evasion. Noah Webster described "darn" as already common in New England in 1789, while "tarnal," "cuss" and "I swan" all came into use in the early days of the Republic. But the majority of frontiersmen, wagoners, circuit riders and politicians preferred their profanity straight and virtually conquered the continent on the combined stength of their "corn likker" and cursing.

The genteel English visitor, Mrs. Trollope, traipsing around the States in 1829, remarked upon the American fondness for "that most unfailing expletive 'God D-mn' " and gave up counting the number of times she heard it after the first entry in her Notebook: "17 times within hearing." Lacking any more complete record of the way men swore in reality, the student of nineteenth-century profanity is left largely to his own surmises. "The language of the street is always strong," Emerson hints in his journal of 1840. "And I confess to some pleasure from the stinging rhetoric of a rattling oath in the mouth of truckman and teamster. How laconic and brisk it is by the side of a page from the *North American Review*. Cut these words and they would bleed; they are vascular and alive; they walk and run."

Surely the philosopher was not referring to such bloodless bombast as Melville used to convey the salty flavor of Captain Peleg's speech in *Moby Dick:* "Flukes and flames! Bildad, say that again to me, and start my soul-bolts, but I'll—, I'll—, yes, I'll swallow a live goat with all his hair and horns on. Out of the cabin, ye canting, drab-colored son of a wooden gun . . . !"

This, one suspects, is party-dress profanity, calculated to suggest the genuine article without disturbing the sensibilities of schoolmarms and prigs. When the novel's seagoing narrator, Ishmael, blurts "Gracious!" the call of the mild comes through like a shrill, girlish squeak.

Throughout the nineteenth century the treasury of tepid "cuss" words increased. "Hell" became *heck*, *blazes* or *thunder*. "Damn" became *drat*, *darn*, *blast*, *blame* or *bother*. "Goddamn" was amended to *goshdarn*, *doggone*, *goldarn*, *consarn*, *dad-blame*, *dad-burn* and the like. *Lawsy*, *lawdy*, *land* and *lawks* were used in place of "Lord." "God" was reduced to *gosh*, *golly*, *great Scott*, *good grief*, *great guns* and *good gravy*. "Jesus" became *gee-whiz*, *jiminy*, *jeez*, *Jerusalem*, *Jehosophat* and *gee-whillikers*. "Christ" was *cripes*, *cracky*, *Christopher* and *Christmas*, while the Savior's full name was rendered as *jiminy crickets*, *Judas' priest*, *John Jacob Astor* or *G. Rover Cripes*. Too obvious for discussion are the literal four-letter meanings that lurk behind such old folksy subterfuges as *Pish!*, *Shoot!*, *Piffle!*, *Shucks!*, *Pshaw!* and *Fudge!*

Writing in London, the spiritual capital of the Nice-Nelly movement, Gilbert and Sullivan lyrically lampooned the hypocrisy of the age in the boast of the Captain of the *Pinafore:*

Bad language or abuse,
I never, never use,
Whatever the emergency;
Though "Bother it" I may
Occasionally say,
I never use a big, big D—
ALL: *What, never?*
CAPTAIN: *No, never!*
ALL: *What,* never?
CAPTAIN: *Hardly ever!*
ALL: *Hardly ever swears a big, big D—*

To judge from the deluge of complaints written to the London *Telegraph*, however, big D's and little d's—as well as H's, F's, B's and S.O.B.'s—were very much a part of the actual Victorian vocabulary. As one correspondent claimed: "There is not a delicate ear that is not daily outraged by the unspeakable blasphemies and hideous indecencies of London language, particularly on Sunday, when lounging, loafing, and idling are prevalent . . . "

Of course, ladies and gentlemen with delicate ears could always spend Sunday at home with a good clean book, such as *The Family Shakespeare*, from which Thomas Bowdler had thoughtfully cut—or "bowdlerized"—every jot and tittle of profanity. Going their Puritan ancestors one better, proper Victorians had a new Standard English word to suppress—"bloody"—a word which Julian Sharman, England's Victorian historian of profanity, described as "the crown and apex of all bad language," surpassing "in vileness and intensity anything of the kind that has been intense or vile."

Unable to account for British aversion to this strangely decent indecency, Americans erroneously linked it to menstruation. Equally at a loss, some etymologists suggested derivations from " 'Sblood" and "by Our Lady," while others traced it to the Crimean War and the Russian word for "obscene," *bliudi*. Most plausible, however, was the theory that it was merely a translation of the German *blutig*, or "bloody," which English troops picked up during sixteenth-century campaigns in the Low Countries. It was used for hundreds of years as a superlative, as in "bloody hot" or "bloody cold," and its infamous reputation can be attributed only to the supersqueamishness of nineteenth-century prudes, who were reluctant to admit that they had bodies, much less pulses that throbbed with a warm "sanguine fluid."

Bloody well aware of its sensational value, George Bernard Shaw wrote the word into *Pygmalion* for Mrs. Pat Campbell, who played Eliza Doolittle. A *New York Times* review of the London opening reported that the word was "waited for with trembling, heard shudderingly." "Not bloody likely," Mrs. Campbell muttered to the thrilled house, and Shaw had a hit on his hands. As euphemisms, the English used "ruddy" and "blooming"—the latter appearing in a tag line of *My Fair Lady*, when the modern musical Eliza shocks the Ascot racing toffs by shouting to a horse, "Come on, Dover! Move your bloomin' arse!"

Though "bloody" never took hold in America, its acceptance in Australia was such that it became known as "The Great Australian Adjective," and Robert Graves has quoted it with suitable British blanks in an "Australian Battle Hymn" of World War I:

Gird yer——loins up, get yer——gun,
Set the——enermy an' watch him——run.
Git a——move on, have some——sense,
Learn the——art of self de——fence!

With the dashes transposed into the key of F, the song might have passed for American or English during World War II, when our modern version of the old Sanskrit *fukshan* became the "crown and apex of all bad language" on both sides of the Atlantic. By 1941 "bloody" had become so worn with use that it even managed to slip into the pages of the London *Times*. "Clashing her wiry old ringlets in a kind of palsied glee at her own audacity, Auntie *Times* has printed a little poem containing the line 'I really loathe the *bloody* Hun,'" D. B. Wyndham Lewis reported in the *Tatler*. "Don't say we didn't warn you if Auntie is seen dancing down Fleet Street ere long in her red flannel undies, bawling little French songs."

Meanwhile, Uncle Sam was wagging his whiskers at the increasing vogue for tabooed expletives in American writing. As Cole Porter had tunefully observed, authors who once knew better words now only used four-letter words writing prose. Anything went—at least in the novel—and being banned in Boston was better than a dozen rave reviews. Asked to name a single book responsible for this reversal of the American attitude toward literary profanity, pundits are prone to pick Joyce's *Ulysses*. Closer to home and more influential, perhaps, was Owen Wister's best seller of 1902, *The Virginian*, in which swearing received its first popular support in the twentieth century. "You're such a son-of-a—— when you get down to work," the Virginian's old pal Steve says with an affectionate grin. "I expected he would be struck down," the novel's narrator confides. "He had used to the Virginian a term of heaviest insult . . . Evidently he had meant no harm by it, and evidently no offence had been taken. Used thus, the language was plainly complimentary."

An uncomplimentary use of the same term in a later scene gave the nation a catch phrase that survives to this day. "Your bet, you son-of-a——," the cowardly Trampas growled during a game of "cyards" at the local saloon. "The Virginian's pistol came out, and his hand lay on the table, holding it unaimed. And with a voice gentle as ever . . . he issued his orders to the man Trampas: 'When you call me that, *smile!*' "

A little more than two decades later, Broadway audiences not only smiled but roared laughter at the third-act tag line of Ben Hecht's and Charles MacArthur's *The Front Page:* "The son of a bitch stole my watch!" The second-act curtain had rung down with an equally blatant "God damn it," and it seemed as though the blankety blanks had been filled in for all time.

By 1935, Depression-inspired dramas of social significance were using swearing in some of their more tender love scenes and Sidney Kingsley's *Dead End* kids were bringing a new naturalness of expression to the stage. "Oh, so you're the one!" Tommy's sister, Dina, shouts angrily at Spit. "Come on!"

SPIT (*thumbs his nose*): Like hell I will.
DINA: Come on!
SPIT: Frig you!
DINA (*flaring*): I'll crack you . . . you talk like that!
SPIT: Ah, I'll sock yuh inna tit.

Dina smacks him, and an argument erupts between Tommy and Spit. "Ah, yuh mudduh's chooch!" Spit snarls. To which Tommy retorts, "Ah, yuh fadduh's doop!"

"They're really horrible brats," an outraged dowager comments at one point. "And their language!"

"Ah, shut up, yuh fat bag a hump!" Tommy mutters. And, when a gentleman with glasses intervenes, the manly little chap responds with a shouted, "Balls to yew, faw eyes!"

This was swearing such as most city dwellers could have heard by opening a window. Sprinkled with Old World exotics, like the Italian "Fongoola!" and the Yiddish "Gay cock of'm yam!," it possessed a vitality that was missing in the Spanish-type swearing Hemingway used a little later in *For Whom the Bell Tolls:*

" 'Thy duty,' said Augustín mockingly. 'I besmirch the milk of thy duty.' Then turning to the woman, 'Where the un-nameable is this vileness that I am to guard?'

" 'In the cave,' Pilar said. 'In two sacks. And I am tired of thy obscenity.'

" 'I obscenity in the milk of thy tiredness,' Augustín said.

" 'Then go and befoul thyself,' Pilar said to him without heat."

More chitchat follows, and more unswearing. "Daughter of the great whore of whores," Augustín obscenities. "I befoul myself in the milk of the springtime."

"Pilar slapped him on the shoulder.

" 'You,' she said, and laughed that booming laugh. 'You lack variety in your cursing. But you have force. Did you see the planes?'

" 'I un-name in the milk of their motors,' Augustín said . . .

" 'That's something,' Pilar said. 'That is really something. But really difficult of execution.'

" 'At that altitude, yes,' Augustín grinned. '*Desde luego*. But it is better to joke.' "

One might venture the opinion that it is also better to swear outright. Here is euphemism with a difference, and even the tragic young American, Robert Jordan, is affected. "Oh, muck my grandfather and muck this whole treacherous muck-faced mucking country and every mucking Spaniard in it," he mentally mock swears, until the reader feels inclined to second Augustín's suggestion: "Go to the unprintable . . . And unprint thyself."

The device can hardly be attributed to literary flinching, since Hemingway had already proven himself a rugged four-letter man in *Death in the Afternoon*. As an attempt at achieving freshness, the experiment was indeed worth while—particularly in view of later War II novels, in which the sheer repetition of armed-forces profanity creates a kind of armchair combat fatigue. When one of Norman Mailer's Marines sinks to the ground and mumbles, "Fug the sonofabitchin' mud," the word-weary reader collapses by his side.

" 'Get up,' somebody would cry.

" 'Fug you. Fug the goddam gun.' "

As far back as 1933, the late George Orwell neatly nutshelled both the nature and the predicament of modern profanity. "The whole business of swearing, especially English swearing, is mysterious," he wrote. "Of its very nature swearing is as irrational as magic—indeed, it is a species of magic. But there is also a paradox about it, namely this: Our intention in swearing is to shock and wound, which we do by mentioning something that should be kept secret—usually something to do with the sexual functions. But the strange thing is that when a word is well-established as a swear word, it seems to lose its original meaning; that is, it loses the thing that made it into a swear word."

Because of this law of diminishing indecency, sexual profanity has lost much of its punch. "Womb to tomb!" and "Sperm to worm!" are *West Side Story*'s death-wishful equivalents of the Dead End kids' fertility-laden invocations of "yuh mudduh's chooch!" and "yuh fad-duh's doop!" The fighting words are no longer "son of a bitch" and "bastard" but "Spic!," "Wop!," "Mick!" and "Garlic-mouth!"

This is the billingsgate of bigotry, the new profanity of prejudice, whose sting and bite paradoxically derive from the efforts of the enlightened to make such words taboo. In the melting-pot atmosphere of fifty years ago, names like "Wop," "Yid," "Hunkie" and "Mick" had little power to shock or wound and were freely bandied about. Writing in *Show Biz* of the influx of Chinese restaurants into the Times Square area after World War I, Abel Green and Joe Laurie, Jr., recall that "in those uninhibited days, *Variety* thought nothing of calling them chink joints and using terms like 'yellow peril,' whereas today, if reference to Irving Berlin's origin as a catch-penny singing waiter in Nigger Mike's place on the Bowery comes up, the joint is just referred to as Mike's. Hebe comedians, tad [Irish] comics and Yonny-Yonson-type jokes were terms devoid of politico connotations . . . "

Times have changed, however, and sociopolitical

swearing has become the deadliest of all. Among its dirty words are such sure-fire hostility arousers as "Fascist," "Red," "Nigger-lover," "Jew-baiter," "Uncle Tom," "scab," "subversive," "reactionary," "pinko" and the like. Milder and less offensive are such secular vagaries as "huckster," "egghead," "beatnik," "square," "oddball," "weirdo," "queer" and a host of other scurrilities denoting social or sexual deviation.

Obviously, these are of limited use and would be inappropriate when applied to the average, everyday son of a bitch. For want of new and more universal creations, therefore, the supply of American swearwords has become seriously limited and even Tennessee Williams' hot-tin-roof types are reduced to borrowing. "What is it Big Daddy always says when he's disgusted?" Big Mama asks.

BRICK: Big Daddy says "crap" when he's disgusted.
BIG MAMA: That's right—*CRAP!* I say *CRAP* too, like Big Daddy!

The fact that Jack Gelber's play, *The Connection*, brought CRAP's noneuphemistic and excretory original into the theater as the narcotic addicts' pet name for heroin changes nothing. With Mamas and Daddies of all sizes swearing each other's hand-me-down oaths, profanity has become chained to a parrot perch and the dedicated swearer of the old blue-streak school is left wondering, "What the #&%@! is the future of swearing?"

In an entertaining and erudite attempt at an answer, Robert Graves has essayed the opinion that modern profanity has no future—at least none worthy of its past. But we cannot yet bring ourselves to accept this gloomy prognosis. Though the mainstream of Anglo-American swearing has thinned to a dull trickle, the wellsprings of Asiatic swearing still bubble with a vitality from which the word-parched Westerner may imbibe fresh inspiration.

"May wild asses browse on your grandmother's grave! . . . May the principles of your warmth and cold never be properly adjusted; may hate defile your ancestral tablets; and may your hamstrings snap in the moment of achievement!" Such is the elixir of the East, a heady draught of lively spirits concocted with infinite care. To our own flat and ineffectual "go to hell," the most prosaic Siamese swearer adds a few jiggers of personal imagination. "Go to hell" is only the beginning of the curse—the preface to a painstaking description of innumerable custom-tailored tortures, followed by a fervent wish that the offending party will be condemned to "carry water over the flames in a wicker basket to assuage the thirst of the eternal judge, then that he migrate into the body of a slave for as many years as there are grains of sand in four seas, and after this that he may be born a beast for five hundred generations and a hermaphrodite for five hundred more."

In India the ancient art involves the accursed one's whole family, his ancestors, heirs and assigns. "O you father of sixty dogs!" the irate Mohammedan shouts to the driver of a stalled cart. "May your daughter be wedded to a jinn and give birth to three-headed serpents!" If time permits—and it usually does—Hindus engage in a full-scale exchange of curses in *crab-bat*, a language comprising all the swearwords known to Hindustani, plus a choice selection from the more esoteric dialects. For a report on one such brouhaha between an aged cleaning boy and his assistant, we are indebted to Robert Graves, who quotes the account from Frank Richards' *Old Soldier Sahib:*

"First the cleaning boy let loose his broadside, and banged away until he temporarily ran out of ammunition. Then his opponent replied, with shot for shot. . . . They each went along the other's pedigree, generation by generation, making more and more loathsome discoveries, until our cleaning boy was finally acclaimed the victor. He had gone back two thousand years in his rival's genealogical line and given convincing proof that a direct female ancestress had secretly cohabited for years during her widowhood with a diseased bullfrog, thus going one better than her mother, who had legitimately married and cohabited with a healthy pig."

To be sure, few swearing sahibs of Cincinnati, Pocatello and points west enjoy sufficient leisure to cultivate such pukka profanity. But it is possible that new sources of swearing power might be had by harnessing some of the many folk idioms imported to our shores from Europe.

The Irish, fleeing a potato famine, were never starved for words and brought with them a wealth of expostulations besides "begorra," "faith" and "bejabbers": "By all the ten legions of divils of Killooly! . . . By St. Boogar and all the saints at the backside door of Purgatory! . . . By the nineteen balls of the twelve apostles! . . . By the holy St. Mackerel, the high heels of St. Patrick, and the ripping, roaring, jumping Jerusalem!"

Rich in imagery and ageless in spirit are the great Yiddish curses, of which the beautifully succinct "Drop dead!" (or "Get killed!") is but a paltry sample. Consider, for instance, the depth and vigor of such oral masterpieces as "A black ear on your head! . . . May you suffer a burning pain in your seventh liver! . . . May all your teeth ache top and bottom so they have to be pulled by a one-armed blacksmith! . . . You should grow like an onion with your head in the ground forever!"

As Maurice Samuel has pointed out in *The World of Sholom Aleichem*, Yiddish cursing is as much a pastime as an implement of war—a form of self-expression that is often humorous in intent.

Though the history of swearing is long, the need for such sportive curses has only recently been recognized, and *The New York Times* made a 1960 headline of the belated discovery that "SOME ARE FOUND TO CURSE FOR JOY."

The gist of the story was that a British psychologist named Helen E. Ross spent three weeks in Arctic Norway counting the curses of a group of male zoologists who were "studying the effects of continuous daylight on birds' diurnal rhythms." Measuring "the rise and fall of swearing against the rise and fall of the zoologists' spirits," the lady scientist found that the "amount of swearing increased noticeably when people were relaxed and happy." Furthermore, "there appeared to be two types of swearing; 'social swearing,' intended to be friendly and a sign of being 'one of the gang,' and 'annoyance swearing,' when someone really has something to swear about."

"Swearing of the 'social' type was at its height when everything appeared rosy," the *Times* reported. "The 'annoyance' swearing rose as tension and discomfort rose, but dropped off abruptly to 'anti-social silence' when people found the physical and spiritual going really rough."

Thawing out these cold, hard facts from Arctic Norway, it would seem that we now have a whole puddle of fresh possibilities for the future, namely: *Fun with Profanity. The Power of Positive Cursing. Swear Along with Mitch, Moe, Eddie and all the gang, while studying the daily habits of the human-type birds around you.* If new words are lacking, swearing may yet make a happy comeback by adopting a merry mood!

For old-style "annoyance" swearers, who refuse to lapse into "anti-social silence," we can offer no better advice than that of the ancient Chinese: "Be careful whom you swear at: to swear at a man who has justly earned a reputation for virtue and integrity is to make yourself ridiculous; to swear at a man of no reputation at all is to honor him by assuming that he has one. The most suitable victim is someone a little more virtuous than yourself, but with vices differing from your own; if, for example, you are a drunkard or glutton, choose one who is a gambler and frequenter of brothels, and contrariwise. Avoid any appearance of passion. . . . Begin with a great show of courtesy so that he does not suspect your intentions, then gradually unmask your fire. . . . The highest art of swearing consists in thus bringing your opponent to a dead stop. His color will go from pale to red, from red to purple, from purple to ashen. When you have reached this point, stop, otherwise the bystanders will regard you as a bully . . . "

And, shucks, you wouldn't want that to happen, would you?

VI

DANCING

Dancing

With the possible exception of swearing, no form of human expression has occasioned quite so much moral indignation as has dancing. From the "naughty" waltz and the "scandalous" polka to the latest variation on the twist, the advent of each new dance has been the cue for tongue-clucking disapproval and pronouncements of decadence and doom. Only when dancing has lost its original spontaneity and vigor does it cease to be a raffish trollop of the times and become the noble "Mother of all the Arts."

Despite the dainty tutus and tip-toe refinement of coffee-table picture albums devoted to the esthetic glories of The Dance, the history of dancing is, for the most part, riotously earthy, physical and vulgar. In Dryden's definition, dancing is "the poetry of the foot." With equal accuracy it might also be described as the limericks of the legs, the jingles of the arms, the sonnets of the sacroilium or the ballads of the belly and buttocks.

Through the ages, Man's every muscle, limb and fiber has wiggled, jiggled and jumped in dancing celebrations of victory, puberty, birth, marriage, divorce, circumcision, the changes of the moon and the rising of the sun. At various periods and places dances of the feet, neck, eyes, knees, lips, shoulders, thighs, breasts, torso, hands and fingers have been used to promote fertility, ward off devils, worship gods, prepare for war, and make rain, magic, money and whoopee.

The human desire to dance is basic: Man and his universe are all rhythm. The stars and galaxies move in an eternal ballet. The atom is a microscopic ballroom where particles swing and jitter to the frenetic jazz of energy and matter. Respiration is the rhythmic dance of breath, and the heart of the human embryo throbs in double-time syncopation with the maternal pulse. Upon birth, the infant is rocked and nursed at its mother's breast in what the psychiatrist Joost A. M. Meerloo calls the "Milk Dance." "The sucking is rhythmic," he observes; "mother and child move together up and down in a rhythmic way while by another innate reflex action both arms and hands of the child make a pumping movement. In the Far East," he adds, "I experienced several times this rhythmic encounter of mother and baby as a joyous play, full of erotic overtones."

Similar overtones of the erotic are present in all human dances, from the most primitive to the most decorous and polished, and spring directly from nature. The mating dances of whooping cranes, crested grebes, pheasants, moths, butterflies and other winged amorists are counted among the major events of bird and bug watching and have been used to support the theory that bird nests—the earliest known form of architecture—"may first have arisen as an accidental result of the ecstatic sexual dance of birds."

The urge to dance has also been noted in higher animals, such as anthropoid apes, who will shuffle and stamp around a pole or tree for hours. The German psychologist Wolfgang Köhler, who once made a study of such monkeyshines, reports that "In these dances the chimpanzee likes to bedeck his body with all sorts of things, especially strings, vines and rags that dangle and swing in the air"—thus displaying a sense of chic that compares with that of the primitive girl dancers depicted in the earliest Spanish cave painting of a human circle dance: Here Miolithic maidens are seen dancing in a ring around a male youth whose maleness is emphasized by what has been described as "a large but not ithyphallic membrum." Though prehistorians disagree as to the precise nature of this Stone Age shindig, the dance is almost identical with those performed at initiation ceremonies by many primitive peoples today. In some instances the women of the tribe dance around the pubescent young men, and in others the men dance around the newly nubile maidens. In Central Australia, we are told, "the women dance with their arms flexed and make inviting movements," while on the Island of Nauru, in the Pacific, the first menstruation of a chieftain's daughter is celebrated with a dance in which both sexes "raise their grass skirts in front and behind and exhibit themselves to each other."

Simplest of all such dances are the erotic hoedowns of East African tribes, in which girl debutantes mimic the movements of coitus. Among the more complex coming-of-age routines is that of the Monumbo Papuans of New Guinea, who use the dance to instruct young tribal bucks in the responsibilities of manhood—the more mentionable of which include injunctions to "steal diligently, and not let themselves be seen by the women . . . catch fish diligently with the fish spear . . . fetch down cocoanuts and drink the milk from them . . . fetch down breadfruits with pickers and foot-slings . . . delight in women" and "secretly watch the women bathing."

As if this weren't enough to keep a young man out of mischief, most primitive societies demand his presence at numerous other dance rites of an extremely energetic and lascivious sort. In the scholarly estimate of the musicologist and dance historian Curt Sachs, "It would be difficult to imagine the motions of onanism and cohabitation, the suggestion of enormous sexual organs, and the exposure of their own, the frenzied shrieking of obscene words, and the chants of unprintable verses which the dancers of both sexes of the various cultures alone or in couples bring to their dances." By way of restrained example, he cites the spring fertility dances of the Watchandi of Western Australia, who cavort around a large trench "decorated with bushes in such a way as to resemble the sex parts of a woman. In the dance they carry in front of them a spear to represent a phallus. Circling around the ditch, they poke the spear inside as a symbol of generative power, and sing continually, 'not the pit, not the pit, not the pit, but the vulva!' "

In contrast we have an anthropological report on the male-oriented sex hops of the Cobéua Indians of Brazil, whose dancers "have large phalli made of bast with testicles of red cones from the low-hanging trees, which they hold close to their bodies with both hands. Stamping with the right foot and singing, they dance at first in double quick time, one behind another, with the upper parts of their bodies bent forwards. Suddenly they jump wildly along with violent coitus motions and loud groans of '*ai* (*ye*)—*ai* (*ye*)—*ai* (*ye*)' . . . . Thus they carry the fertility into every corner of the houses, to the edge of the woods, to the nearby fields; they jump among the women, young and old, who disperse shrieking and laughing . . ."

Though few instances can be found of the sexual act being consummated as part of the choreography, the fertility dance is always and everywhere the prelude to intercourse—which often follows any other sort of primitive dance as well. In the tribal mind, human potency and fertility are symbolic of health, abundance and victory over the forces of death and destruction. For this reason, fertility, war and funeral dances are more or less interchangeable and anthropologists are often hard put to classify a given set of jumps, shuffles and grunts. From what has been learned, however, it's safe to assume that every step, leap, movement and contortion known to modern dancing had found its way into the primitive repertoire long before man emerged into the Bronze Age.

Because the well-being of the entire tribe was believed to depend upon the perfection of its dance rituals, special skills were highly prized and errors severely punished. Legend has it that until quite recently the elders of Gaua, in the New Hebrides, came to the dance armed with bows and arrows and shot to kill any dancer who weakened the magic potency of the dance by so much as a single mistake. Under such exacting demands, dancing tended to become the full-time career of a professional caste, as it did in India, where temple dancers have traditionally dedicated their lives to the worship of dancing gods.

In his essay on *The Art of Dancing*, Havelock Ellis noted that Indian Devidasis, or sacred dancing girls, are formally wedded to male divinities, "and their dances represent the life of the god they are married to as well as the emotions of love they experience for him." Other sources attest to the fact that such marriages are by no means purely mystical. When a dancing girl blossoms into young womanhood, "the stone phallus of the God Siva takes her virginity, and with this act she enters into the possession of the priests who are the representatives of the god."

For all their aesthetic complexity, the dances of India still reveal a strong undercurrent of the erotic. The most widely known of those that have survived from former ages is the *Karshni*, performed by eight milkmaids who dance in a circle around the flute-bearing god Krishna in the same manner in which women of the Stone Age danced around the youth with the large male membrum. Among others described by the modern authority Projesh Banerji are the *Jakhari*, "the dance which flushed the women and men of Turkey bearing bouquets, performed in amorous moods," and dances which portray the temptation of Indra's son by the voluptuous and beautiful Apsarases—heavenly nymphs who "perform various evolutions, shaking their deep bosoms and casting glances around . . ."

Though divided into four regional types, all Indian dances developed from the same ancient source, and their every step and gesture is codified in the pages of the *Natya Sastra*—a book which is believed to contain the dance secrets of the gods. "When the neck is moved backward and forward like the movement of a she-pigeon's neck, it is called *Prakampita.* Usage: To denote 'You and I,' folk-dancing, swinging, inarticulate murmurings and the sound uttered by a woman at the time of conjugal embrace." The hand held in one position conveys no less than thirty possible meanings, including "short man," "the massage of wrestlers," "holding the breasts of women," "saying 'It is proper' " and "the flapping of elephant ears." When the dancer's third finger is doubled under the thumb, it may be construed as "flower," "screw pine," "the union of man and woman" or "rubbing down a horse."

Over countless centuries, the Indian dance has perfected thirty-nine such significant hand gestures and forty-five eloquent eye movements, in addition to a numerous variety of postures, gaits, steps, jumps and psychic conditions. All serve the purpose of storytelling dance dramas whose influence has spread through Asia to the islands of the South Seas, where the myths and legends told by a hula dancer's hands form a graceful counterpoint to her swaying hips and undulating torso. To the untutored eye of the mainland American, the story elements of the Hawaiian hula are considerably less interesting than the febrile footnotes of the dancer's pelvis, which speaks the same international language of *l'amour* that grandfather learned at carnival peep shows under the spangle-tossing tutelage of some itinerant Little Egypt. Curiously, however, the Egyptians themselves are supposed to have learned the ancient belly dance from watching another group of traveling artistes: the bevies of bumping and grinding Hindu dancing girls who were brought to the Land of the Pharaohs in 1500 B.C. as part of the sensual spoils of war with kingdoms of the East.

"It is interesting to note," Havelock Ellis commented, "that Egypt still retains, almost unchanged, through fifty centuries, its traditions, technique, and skill in dancing, while as in ancient Egyptian dancing, the garment forms an almost or quite negligible element of the art." In this respect, it is also interesting to note that the high kicks of the modern chorus line are first seen in a relief carving of 2500 B.C., in which rows of Egyptian chorines, clad in transparent gauze, execute an *en masse* leg throw that exactly duplicates the high precision kicks of the Radio City Music Hall Rockettes.

Kicks, leaps and lively running steps were second nature to the Egyptians, to whom the word *hbj*, or "dance," also meant "to be joyful." At royal festivals in the Old Kingdom, even the lords of the Nile leaped and nimbly frolicked, while ladies of the court sat in with the musicians to play cymbals, tambourines and castanets. Above all other prizes of war, the Egyptians cherished African Pygmies, whose remarkable dancing abilities were put to the service of the gods and Pharaohs. To this day, Pygmy tribal dancers are noted for their spectacular one-legged jumps and realistic imitations of animals and birds. These were a natural complement to religious dances in which the ancient Egyptians wore falcon masks, and they echoed prehistoric cave paintings in which dancers are disguised as animals for the magic rites that set the precedent for later masquerade balls.

Spectacular, too, were Egyptian backbends and the whirling dances which predated the hour-long trance dance of the Moslem "whirling dervishes." Such spinning dances were prevalent throughout the Middle East. Assyrian soldiers of the seventh century B.C. reportedly "whirled themselves like tops," and the ancient Hebrew name for the dancing of women derives from the verb for "turn"—as in a whirlwind or the swinging of a sword.

Both the Talmud and the Old Testament testify to the fact that the ancient Hebrews danced for joy and the glory of the Lord. King David danced before the Ark of the Covenant, and when the children of Israel had safely crossed over out of Egypt, Miriam the prophetess "took a timbrel"—or tambourine—"in her hand; and all the women went out after her with timbrels and with dances." Easily the most sensational dance in Biblical history was the one performed by Salome at Herod's birthday party—a dance which so pleased Herod that "he promised with an oath to give her whatsoever she would ask." Salome, at her mother's urging, requested and got John the Baptist's head. Her dance, which Victorian poets were prone to interpret as a pretty twinkling of the feet, was, according to all earlier evidence, nothing more or less than a *danse du ventre*, or Eastern belly dance.

Salome aside, the belly dance was far from typical of the Jewish people, whose gay, skipping courtship dances were of the sort which "the daughters of Jerusalem went forth and danced in the vineyards." An equally idyllic dance is described in the *Iliad* as characteristic of the Homeric Greeks: "There were youths dancing, and maidens of costly wooing, their hands upon one another's wrists. . . . And now would they run around with deft feet exceeding lightly . . . And now anon they would run in lines to meet each other. And a great company stood round the lovely dance in joy; and among them a divine minstrel was making music on his lyre, and through the midst of them, leading the measure, two tumblers whirled."

To the poet Pindar, Hellas was "the land of lovely dancing," and modern dance critics still invoke the name of the Greek muse Terpsichore in their reviews of "terpsichorean" performances. But it would be erroneous to imagine that Hellenic dances were all graceful leaps and toe steps. In addition to the ancient Etruscan squatting dance, the Greeks also enjoyed hand-clapping, thigh-slapping dances which reached their peculiar peak in the *rhathapygizein*—a rowdy, fanny-slapping quickstep in which girl soloists kicked their own bare buttocks pink with the soles of their dainty feet.

Other crowd-pleasers were the *gymnopaidiai*, in which naked young men danced intricate wrestling movements, and war dances in which soldiers mimicked an actual battle. It was Socrates' opinion that the best dancers made the best warriors, and Sophocles danced in the chorus of his own dramas in order to strengthen his sense of the poetic meters—all of which had their origins in the dance and are still described in terms of "feet." The spondee, with its foot of two long syllables, takes its name from the solemn dance which accompanied a *sponde*, or drink offering to the gods. The trochee was once the tripping *trochaios*, and poems written in the meter of bawdy Bacchic hymns are "ithyphallic," in allusion to the huge phallus that was carried in dancing processionals at the festival of the wine god.

Facsimiles of the *membrum virile erectus* were standard equipment for erotic satyr dances performed by trios comprising one man and two women and were worn like souvenir badges at the Bacchanalia, where drunken male celebrants danced lasciviously around ecstatic *maenads*—the sacred "mad women" of the Dionysian cult. In imperial Rome, where dancing embraced every erotic movement and gesture conceivable to the human imagination, the Bacchanalia became wild, drunken sex brawls. Contrary to popular belief, however, such erotic binges were not always typical of Rome and represent a rather late development. The Romans were, for the most part, the hard-working executives of antiquity—administrators, engineers, generals and lawyers—whose lack of frivolous imagination is evident in early choral dances in which two groups of older and younger men stamped tirelessly around in circles, beating a businesslike rhythm on shields. Indeed, the only exhibition dancing that really appealed to the old Roman aristocracy was the storytelling gesture dance of the mimes, whose techniques and traditions were borrowed from the Greek theater. But as spectacles and circuses became bigger and more gory under each succeeding Caesar, the pantomime adopted crime and horror formats and farces were laced with erotic ballets performed by women dancers who disrobed during the course of the play in a sort of integrated strip tease. Their pelvic grinds and breast vibrations were cheered by plebs and tired businessmen, while Juvenal reports that women were aroused by lewd dances of the kind used to express Pasiphaë's lust for intercourse with a bull. "Tuccia cannot contain herself," he wrote. "Your Apulian maiden heaves a sudden and longing cry of ecstasy as though she were in a man's arms; the rustic Thymele is all attention, she learns her lesson." That such lessons were well learned by rustic and patrician Urb alike we gather from Ovid's description of "The Loves":

One is a dancer, swaying, the perfect picture of rhythm,
Movements luring my heart with the seduction of art.

Let the most stoical of men witness her dance, he cries, and "Straightway before your eyes, what a Priapus will rise!"

The reaction of the early Church was one of righteous wrath and condemnation. Converted to Christianity after a dissolute youth, Augustine, the sainted Bishop of Hippo, declared, "The dance is a circle with the devil in the center." But when people refused to give up their old fertility frolics, the church fathers sought to make the dance symbolic of the joyous afterlife to come, when, in the words of Clement of Alexandria, "thou shalt dance in a ring together with the Angels, around Him Who is without beginning or end." On saints' days, ceremonial dancing was often conducted within the church, and lively funeral dances around the churchyard celebrated the rebirth of the dead in Paradise. Since secular dancing was frowned upon as pagan, dancing in graveyards became a favorite outlet for peasants of the Dark Ages. The people were haunted by fears of plague, famine and war, and their dancing was often obsessive. Epidemics of uncontrollable dancing broke out in towns and villages and have been attributed to mass hysteria, nervous disorders due to a disease of the rye used in bread, and *chorea major*—a neurological ailment which laymen still call "St. Vitus's dance" in honor of the patron saint whose influence was sought in prayers for the afflicted. Regardless of causes or cures, the grotesque "dancing mania" became associated in the minds of clergymen, poets and painters with the eternal Dance of Death, and church murals showed skeletons and mortals linked arm in arm in a *danse macabre*.

One theory has it that the word "macabre" was imported into Europe by the Crusaders, who filched the melancholy adjective from the Saracen *makabr*, meaning "graveyards." Less linguistic knights, such as Frederick II of Sicily, brought home gayer baggage in the form of duty-free dancing girls, whom they had picked up in the East to entertain their guests with after-dinner belly dances. To the sensual strains of Arabic dance music within castle walls were added the castanets, tambourines and fiery guitars of wandering gypsy tribes, who danced their way across medieval Europe. It was the gypsies—formerly the "Gipcyans," or "Egyptians"—who kept alive the ancient dance of joy in southern Europe, while peasants of the north danced out their fears and repressions in damp graveyards.

In Provence, where the ideals of love and courtliness were sung by wandering troubadours, aristocrats and nobles formed "courts of love" and danced the *farandole* and *branle*. The branle, also known as the French brawl, was a swaying circle dance, and the farandole was a kind of rhythmic follow-the-leader in which a group of dancers joined hands and gaily tripped through gardens and over meadows to the accompaniment of their own voices. To promote the cause of personalized romance, some unsung genius of Provence conceived the idea of breaking the group up into couples, who would dance side by side, holding hands. Simple as the innovation may sound, its cultural and social effects were far-reaching. Released from the ring and single file, couples were free to dance about in all directions, and castle hearths were moved from the traditional center of the hall to a side wall, in order to permit the maximum of movement. The floor was, in effect, cleared for modern ballroom dancing, and Western music ceased to be a mere accompaniment for the human voice. Instruments now played both melody and harmony, and the first small orchestras were formed—thus paving the way for Debussy and Dixieland, Bach, Benny Goodman, Rachmaninoff and rock 'n' roll.

But all was not joy and harmony. In the thirteenth century Provence became the scene of a bloody religious crusade and the dancing courtiers were virtually exterminated. But a sufficient number of nobles and troubadours escaped to carry the idea of couple dancing to the courts of Germany, Italy, France and England. The dance, which was called the *Estampie Gai*, swept all Europe. Originally a vigorous rustic stomp, it had been refined into a series of graceful steps and glides, which were sometimes danced in trio form, like the satyr dances of ancient Greece. The dance was copied by servants and heavy-booted peasants, who restored its stamping vitality at fetes and frolics on the green. Earthy leaps, swings and steps were added, and from these spirited variations courtly dancing masters created enough new steps and dances to beguile both knights and damsels for the next 500 years.

In the year 1400, ladies in high, pointed hats and heavy trains danced the stately *basse danse* and processional *pavanes* with gentlemen in skintight breech hose and long, pointed shoes. Vigorous movement was impossible, but tender glances and warm kisses were encouraged. As one Italian dancing master put it, such courtesies were indeed "*bellissima* for the lady in every measure of the dance, provided that she goes with swaying and undulating movements of the body in the manner prescribed."

By the middle of the century, Spanish and Italian dancing masters had expanded the kissing-courtship idea into intricate figure dances that pantomimed the joys of both promiscuity and true love. On the one hand, there was *La Mercantia*, in which the woman "conferred her favors upon all, represented by a lady with three gentlemen, one beside her, and two behind." On the other was *La Sobria*, in which the lady conferred her favors upon only one. In Italy such dances were called *balleti*—"little dances," whose amorous themes suggest an early and rudimentary version of the later ballet.

Because of their specialized steps and movements, the mincing *balleti* were described in detail in dance manuals, whereas the most popular dance of the fifteenth century was mentioned only by name. This was the *Morisco*, a Hispano-Moorish dance that seems to have been the main event at every ball and masquerade of the period. As clues to its origin and type, students of the dance cite travelers' descriptions of sumptuous parties in Portugal and Spain, where "women and maidens danced delightfully in the heathen manner." But all such speculations become confused when one must account for the fact that the English Morris (or Moorish) Dance has been performed for centuries by six goose-stepping men, one of whom wears a cardboard horse around his hips and another of whom skips about in the guise of "Mayde Marion."

Uncertain, too, are the origins of the *courante*, which seems to have involved a certain amount of genteel leaping, and the German *Trotto*, which was known in France as the "German," or *Allemande*—a name which still lingers on in the repertoire of American square dance figures. Also alive today are the staccato stamping steps of sixteenth-century Spanish dances, which began with the *Danse des Canaries*, an Old World refinement of a wildly sexual funeral dance which Spanish explorers learned from the grief-stricken native girls of the Canary Islands. Easily the most notorious of all such imports was the Central American *saraband*, a dance of such unparalleled indecency that a Spanish law was passed in 1583 to prevent people from humming its music. In one account, the saraband is described as a dance in which girls with castanets and men with tambourines "exhibit indecency in a thousand positions and gestures. They let the hips sway and the breasts knock together. They close their eyes and dance the kiss and the last fulfillment of love."

Since Spanish dons and dames continued to do the saraband on the sly, dancing masters developed a legal no-knock version which was tame enough to be danced in the courts of southern Europe. Its chief competitor was the *Nizzarda*, an action-packed promenade in which the gentleman made his lady "leap three times in the air" and "with his knee as support, lifts her up high and lets her down again." In the Germanic nations, lady-lifting was practiced by rakes of all ranks, who hoisted their partners aloft by placing their hands intimately beneath the "busk," or corset. Moralists clucked their tongues at the "shameful touching" and clucked again when their *gemütlich* compatriots made the remarkable discovery that couples need not dance side by side but could spin and hop around the floor while locked in a close embrace. The dance, which was called the *volta*, excited the interest of even the most sophisticated Frenchmen. Montaigne, who saw it danced at a ball given by the Fuggers of Augsburg in 1580, remarked that men held their partners so close "that they were cheek to cheek," and Brantôme found the volta delightful to watch, for "by causing the skirts to fly," it always revealed "something pleasing to the sight."

Shakespeare mentions the volta as being popular with the energetic English, who were inclined to treat all dances as a form of physical exercise. The French *gaillard*, for instance, was a high-kicking dance which made even the most fastidious Parisian dandies "sweat exceedingly." As performed in Elizabethan England, however, it became an acrobatic spectacle which made London dancing schools one of the city's chief tourist attractions. Visitors remarked at how wonderfully the dancers "leaped, flung and took on," and Elizabeth herself danced "six or seven galliards" every morning, as part of a personal fitness program.

On a visit to rural Cowdray in 1591, the high-stepping Queen became so bewitched by the robust dancing of the rustics that palace balls were soon enlivened by the sight of elegantly dressed courtiers kicking up their heels in country reels, rounds and quick-time jigs. "In wine we call for bawdy Jiggs . . . rumbillows, whirligigs," an anonymous rhymester wrote in one of the *Roxburghe Ballads*, and on the folk level all sixteenth-century dances were bawdy. Brueghel's Flemish peasants flew around "like wild bears" in the *Hoppeldei*. Germans threw their arms and legs about in the rousing *Gimpel-gampel* and tricked their girls into tumbling over on the grass with skirts thrown over their heads. In a preachment against the ancient English custom of dancing around phallic Maypoles, the Puritan Philip Stubbs piously exclaimed, "What clipping, what culling, what kissing and bussing, what smouching and slabbering one of another, what filthy groping and unclean handling is not practiced at these dancings?" With statistics compiled from puritanical peeps and guesses, he estimated that not one girl in three retained her virginity after taking part in such revels. In short, he thundered, "If you would have your daughter whezith, bawdy and unclean and a filthy speaker and such-like, bring her up in music and dancing . . ."

The Puritans were particularly incensed by dancing on the Sabbath. But many of the rebellious Roundheads were not against dancing on other occasions, and Cromwell himself hired fifty fiddlers to play for dancing at his daughter's wedding. The dances of the Puritan Commonwealth were chaste and class-leveling: group "rounds" that had no leader, bourgeois "Squares for eight" and democratic "Longways sets for as many as will." Smouching and slobbering were out, and the emphasis was on lively English stepping. "Come, and trip it as ye go," the Puritan poet Milton urged, "On the light fantastic toe."

In the New England of America, however, the Puritan step was fantastically heavy. The strait-laced settlers at Plymouth were distressed to find that the Indians not only danced on Sunday but leaped and stamped about "like Anticks." Worse yet, in 1625 one Thomas Morton opened a non-Puritan plantation at Merry Mount with free beer and dancing around an eighty-foot Maypole. In the roaring condemnation that followed, Morton and his men were accused of setting up a "Stynking Idol" and "inviting the Indean women for their consorts, dancing and frisking togither (like so many fairies, or furies, rather), and worse practises," which smacked of "ye madd Bacchanalians!" More moderate opinions were imported from the mother country with the arrival of the Reverend John Cotton, in 1633. "Dancing (yea though mixt) I would not simply condemn," he reasoned with appropriate quotes from Scripture. "Only lascivious dancing to wanton ditties, and amorous gestures and wanton dalliances . . ." The majority soberly agreed, and by the end of the seventeenth century the Puritan penchant for self-improvement led to the recognition of dancing as a social discipline and dancing schools were opened in Boston, where "Grave Persons" taught "Decency of Behavior" to the young.

The self-improvement theme was underscored in the preface to John Playford's *English Dancing Master*—a manual which also found its way into the libraries of the Virginia settlers, who danced purely for pleasure. Fun was also the sole intent of the dancing Dutch at New Amsterdam, where peg-legged Peter Stuyvesant sat beneath a shady tree on Bowling Green to watch the merry Lowland dances, rewarding with "a hearty smack . . . the buxom lass who held out longest and tired down every competitor." According to Diedrich Knickerbocker, the doughty Stuyvesant frowned only once, when a strong breeze lifted a dancer's skirts so high that "a display of the graces took place." Though "averse to meddling with the petticoats of ladies . . . he immediately recommended that every one should be furnished with a flounce at the bottom." The ruling touched off a rebellion among the young *vrouws*, who threatened to leave off their "petticoats altogether; whereupon the good Peter shrugged his shoulders, dropped the subject, and ever after suffered the women to wear their petticoats and cut their capers as high as they pleased . . ."

In France, where country dances were called *contredanses* (because the two lines of participants stood *contre*, or opposite, each other), Charles II of England danced away the days and months of exile while waiting for Cromwell's Commonwealth to collapse. His host, Louis XIV, was even more devoted to dancing and had fathered the French ballet by founding the *Académie Royale de la Danse*, where the five "positions" of the classical ballet were first formulated. Courtiers, who had formerly danced in palace entertainments, were soon displaced by the academy's trained professionals, with the result that the French nobility began to use social dancing as a display of personal expertise. Academic *bourrées*, *rigodons* and *passepieds* became the height of Continental fashion, and even the lively courante was reduced to a technical exercise.

In 1666 Samuel Pepys visited the court of Restoration England and witnessed "Courants" and French dances so "rare" and subtle that they quickly "grew tiresome." The ultimate in spectator boredom was yet to come, however, in the form of the French *minuet*—a folk dance of Poitou which palace dancing masters refined into a pastiche of dainty steps, chivalrous bows and coy curtsies. Lacking both vitality and joy, the minuet proved to be the dancing masters' most lucrative creation—a choreographic clockwork that provided lifetime careers for three generations of snuff-sniffing sycophants. Treatises were written on the proper turning of the wrist. Sixty pages were required to describe the intricacies of the gentleman's bow, and dancing became an exhibition of rhythmic etiquette.

Long before the French Revolution put an end to aristocratic airs and graces, the nobles of Versailles themselves grew weary of the decorous minuet and promptly turned to *contredanses* as soon as the opening minuet had been danced for the sake of form. In colonial America a typical dance program was "first Minuets one Round; Second Giggs; third Reels; and last of all Country Dances." The belief that our forefathers spent their evenings dancing minuets may be attributed largely to Ye-Olde-Tea-Roome-type historical pageants, which depict colonial Americans as superrefined stuffed shirts. Actually, eighteenth-century Americans were among the liveliest dancers in the world, ready to step out with both feet when the fiddles struck up "The Virginia Reel" or "The Devil's Dream." Characteristic in spirit was the famed Philadephia Assembly, which began in 1748 when a group of young bloods hired a warehouse on the Delaware River and solicited subscribers at forty shillings apiece to cover the costs of the orchestra and refreshments. A hogshead of wine and five gallons of rum were needed to keep the punch bowl from running dry, and the wife of the Chief Justice of Pennsylvania arrived at the warehouse on horseback, galloping sidesaddle in a hoop skirt.

Dancing assemblies proved so popular that Congress was unable to curtail them even during the darkest days of the Revolution. With the coming of peace, the victorious General Washington's birthday was celebrated with lavish balls, and General von Steuben recommended that dancing be made a required course for military cadets at West Point. In the aftermath of the French Revolution in 1789, however, many Americans were disturbed by an influx of noble French refugees who set up dancing schools to teach aristocratic steps and manners. "We have a dancing master in town," a patriotic Princeton student wrote in a letter home, "and a fencing master, and I do not know what other animal, but I believe it would be better for us if these frenchmen were all where they came from; for a republick cannot subsist by such useless accomplishments. . . ."

Happily, the "republick" survived both the elegance of the fancy Frenchmen and the worrisome antics of the English-born "Shakers"—a religious sect that shook and jerked the "square-order shuffle" as part of its service of worship. Toward the end of the century, more and more Americans were choosing partners for a secular square-order dance, the *quadrille*, which came to the States by way of England. Books appeared outlining the "figures," and simple "prompts" were called out by a leader at every assembly. The original French terms were given in Anglo-American approximations—and thus *chassé* glided into the language as "sashay" and *dos-à-dos*, or "back-to-back," became the familiar "do-si-do."

Whether held in a backwoods barn or a town hall, dances bred romances, and most American girls were well aware of the necessity to step lively and look pretty. "Nature gave us limbs, and art teaches us to use them," one knowing Philadelphia filly wrote in a letter to the *Minerva* in 1796. Dancing "invigorates the constitution, enlivens the role of the cheek, and in its results operates as silent eloquence upon the hearts of men."

In Germany, lively cheeked *Fräuleins* were rendering their *Herren* blissfully speechless with the eloquence of an invigorating new version of the volatile old volta. Now called the waltz—from *walzen*, meaning "to roll" or "revolve"—the new Danube dance divided the Western world into those who found it an endless delight and those who considered it a source of eternal damnation. For moderns who wonder why the waltz was once called "naughty," history offers an eyewitness report by Ernst Moritz Arndt of the way it was rolled and revolved in 1804 in the vicinity of Erlangen: "The dancers held up the dresses of their partners very high so that they should not trail and be stepped on, wrapped them tightly in this shroud, bringing both bodies under one covering, as close together as possible, and thus the turning went on in the most indecent positions; the hand holding the dress lay hard against the breasts pressing lasciviously at every movement; the girls, meanwhile, looked half mad and ready to swoon. . . ."

Over the protests of aroused moralists, the waltz whirled across Europe in sprightly three-quarter time.

By 1797 it was responsible for the opening of 684 dance halls in Paris alone. " '*Une valse! Oh encore une valse!*' is the constant cry," Arndt reported seven years later. In England, where it was denounced as "the most degenerating dance for more than a hundred years," Byron penned a satiric paean to the "Endearing Waltz," which could "wake to wantonness the willing limbs" and permitted hands to "freely range in public sight." Truth and poetry were wittily mixed in one of the earliest American mentions of the dance, which appeared—surprisingly enough—in the *Boston Weekly Magazine* in 1817:

> *. . . They rise, they twirl, they swing, they fly,*
> *Puffing, blowing, jostling, squeezing,*
> *Very odd, but very pleasing—*
> *'Till every Lady plainly shows*
> *(Whatever else she may disclose)*
> *Reserve is not among her faults:—*
> *Reader, this is to waltz.*

While breast-pressing and skirt-lifting were never official features of the American waltz, the dance still raised the moral neck hair of many social conservatives. "The waltz is a dance of quite too loose a character, and unmarried ladies should refrain from it in public and private," opined *The Gentleman and Lady's Book of Politeness* in 1833. "Very young married ladies, however, may be allowed to waltz in private balls, if it is very seldom and with persons of their acquaintance."

In 1844 Polk was nominated for the Presidency, but

bluenoses of all political tints joined in the hue and cry against a scandalous new foreign dance: the *polka.* Described by one horrified American critic as "a kind of insane Tartar jig," the polka was rumored to be the invention of one Anna Slezakova, a Bohemian peasant girl who improvised its steps out of sheer joy in the early 1830's. Introduced into New York society, the polka became the pet pastime of the American *haut monde* at Newport and Saratoga, where the abandoned display of debutante ankles caused the New York *Herald* to describe the happy hopping dance as one of the most "scandalous exhibitions ever exhibited outside the common gardens of Paris."

The polka was forbidden to be danced in the presence of Queen Victoria and was excluded from all state functions at the White House. Quadrilles were danced at President Lincoln's inaugural ball, but with the firing on Fort Sumter the White House ballroom lights went out and Washington became patriotically austere. As the war dragged on, however, people turned to gay balls and parties for relief from the tedium and tension. There were Enlistment Fund balls and Patent Office balls—and, ultimately, there were Victory balls and peacetime parties at which prominent Washingtonians danced the "Kiss Quadrille." "When it comes to 'swinging corners' each gentleman kisses his partner, and very delightful it must be," the *Rocky Mountain News* reported. "May we be suffered to consider this delicious terpsichorean insanity as a happy augury? In the mad mazes of the political dance . . . are members of Congress to kiss each other?"

If the Kiss Quadrille was ever danced as far west as the Rockies, it was more likely to be known as "Smooch and Swing"—for homesteaders, hillbillies, miners, farmers and cowboys had long since given the quadrille a vital American stamp that was evident in the titles of their "square dance" tunes and figures: "Birdie in a Cage," "Old Arkansaw," "Tumbleweed," "Steal a Little Peek," "Chase the Goose" and "Ladies' Choice—Cheat or Swing." The perfunctory "prompts" of the citified quadrille had become rousing rural "calls" that were often pure folk poetry:

Swing in the center, then break that pair.
Lady goes on and gent stays there.
Once and a half—and now you howl.
Make an arch and shoot the owl!

In the rootin'-tootin' West, the cowboy's swinging partners were most likely to be professional dance-hall girls and lowfalutin ladies of easy virtue, who hustled drinks for the house and doubled in brass beds as prairie prostitutes. But, from all accounts, the most notorious dance dives of the period were in New Orleans, where concert-saloon "waiter-girls" danced the high-kicking *cancan* as it was originally performed in France, with a multitude of fancy flounces and a total absence of pants. Wilder yet was the dancing that went on in the rum-soaked dance halls and barrel houses of the Gallatin Street red-light district. A reporter for the New Orleans *Times*, who took a long, hard look at the low-down hot spots in 1869, found the dancers "in an awful state of nudity." The male patrons were "such a motley throng as Lafitte or any of the pirates of the Gulf might have gathered for their crews. With a piano and two or three trombones for an orchestra, and with dances so abandoned and reckless that the can-can seemed maidenly and respectable, one can form an idea of what the scene was."

Throughout most of the United States and Europe, the female form was bustled out of sight beneath voluminous Victorian skirts and the erotic origins of the dance were being denied or disguised. The "indecent" polka was refined into a modestly gay routine, and the once-"naughty" waltz emerged as the genteel "culmination of modern society dancing." In place of rum-punch assemblies, the socially elect of every major city delighted in champagne balls. The highlight of such occasions was the "cotillion," a gamesy ritual for selecting partners that took its name from a frisky old French folk dance called the *cotillon,* or "petticoat." Popular at New York's suburban Tuxedo Club was the Mirror Cotillion, in which the girl held up a hand mirror and picked her partner from the reflected images of a parade of beaux passing behind her. But this was Cinderella stuff compared to the way the cotillion, or "Parlor German," was handled in the hinterlands. One rural recipe reads: "Six couples up to dance; at signal, the six gentlemen retire to a sawhorse; saw piece of wood, and the one sawing the block in two first waltzes with choice of partners; the last must clean out the muss while leader dances with the lady."

In the Gay Nineties, variety and group fun were the

dancing criteria of the common man, and Jacob Wendall, Jr., gave a rhymed rundown of the major and minor dances of the decade in *The Party at Odd Fellows' Hall:*

Waltzes, polkas, lancers, gallops, glides;
Portland fancy, quadrilles, reels and slides!
High-lows, di-dos, how we danced them all!
I'll never forget that time you may bet,
At the party at Odd Fellows' Hall.

Of all dances, the waltz was still the universal favorite. "Casey would waltz with a strawberry blonde" in 1894 —and twelve years later, in 1906, American blondes, brunettes and redheads were singing, "Waltz me around again, Willie, around and around and around. . . . The music is dreamy, it's peaches and creamy, Oh! don't let my feet touch the ground!"

Early in 1907 the tune suddenly changed, however, and Willie's sweetheart was dancing to a new beat from the band. "I'd Rather Two-Step than Waltz, Bill" expressed the new American preference for a syncopated march tempo that opened the way for the turkey trot, cakewalk and bunny hug. Couples in New York, Chicago, Philadelphia, Boston and San Francisco strutted and stepped to peppy ragtime rhythms that white musicians had borrowed from New Orleans' Negro marching bands. Outraged oldsters bemoaned the fact that young people didn't waltz any more, and professional prudes were quick to trace the relationship between syncopation and sin. The Negro musicians who played in

New Orleans' funeral processions and carnival parades also performed in the brothels of Storyville: they played two-steps for tarts and one-steps for whores and obliged Basin Street "specialty" dancers with renditions of the hootchy-kootchy!

The sin snoopers, who were short on historical perspective, denounced the hootchy-kootchy as a symptom of modern depravity and blamed the bawdy belly dance on "Little Egypt," whose undulating midriff was the main midway attraction of the World's Columbian Exposition at Chicago in 1893. The cooch, as it came to be called, was so basic in its appeal to a generation struggling to break free of Victorian restraints that it was widely imitated by professionals and amateurs alike. In later years, society's Mrs. Nicholas Longworth fondly recalled the night in 1904 when she had scandalized all Newport by dancing "the 'hootchy-kootchy' on Grace Vanderbilt's roof." In London a professional dancer named Maud Allen wiggled her way to world fame by appearing in vaudeville as Salome—complete with harem costume and John the Baptist's head on a platter. Imported to America, the Scriptural squirm was such a success that girl dancers by the hundreds rented prop heads of St. John and set themselves up as Salome acts. Over the next five years, Salomes of all shapes and sizes strove to out-cooch each other. Theaters were raided, Salomes were jiggled off to jail, and burlesque buffs claimed a so-called "first" when a dancer named Odell went all the way by tearing off a strip tease on the stage of the American Theatre in New York in 1907. With the premiere of Richard Strauss's *Salome*, opera fans donned soup-and-fish to ogle Mary Garden's gauzy gyrations in "The Dance of the Seven Veils"—a coloratura cooch which was so mercilessly satirized by Eva Tanguay that vaudeville Salomes began to draw more laughs than applause. Within two years the Salome bit went bust. Dance bands played "Sadie Salome, Go Home," and the shelves of theatrical prop shops were lined with unemployed heads of John the Baptist.

As America swung into 1911 with "Alexander's Ragtime Band," the first furor over the new dances began to die down. The two-stepping maxixe and the snuggle-clutch bunny hug were just beginning to be upgraded from "immoral" to "vulgar" when prudish ears pricked up at the sound of a new double-entendre dance ditty —"Everybody's Doin' It Now!" "Doin' what?" the lyrics asked. "The turkey trot!" Looking back down the years, it's difficult to discover why the energetic one-step caused such an uproar. The reasoning seemed to be that if everybody was doin' it, the turkey trot must be pleasurable, and anything pleasurable that occurred while a man and woman were standing *that* close together must be immoral. Since it was impossible to eradicate the ragtime trot by ranting, pressure was applied wherever stuffiness had the upper hand. One Broadway producer posted a notice that chorus girls caught dancing the turkey trot would be dismissed, and the *Ladies' Home Journal* reportedly fired fifteen girl employees for doin' it during lunch hour. But daytime dancing was on the rise. Housewives were leaving their homes to attend afternoon "tea dansants" in public ballrooms, and department stores combined fashion shows with "Tango Teas."

Denounced by the Federation of Women's Clubs in 1914, the "degrading" tango had already seized Europe in its passionate Latin grip. In London a character played by the glamorous Elinor Glyn took stage center to described how ladies of quality were "clasped in the arms of incredible scum from the Argentine, half-castes from Mexico, and *farceurs* from New York, decadent male things they would not receive in their ante-chambers before this madness set in." In America a wave of adultery suits and blackmail scandals alerted hard-working hubbies to the fact that many wives were receiving ballroom gigolos in their bedchambers for two-timing tango matinees. Militant noises were made, and most middle-class dance palaces dropped the afternoon dansants in the interest of preserving the American home.

Tea dancing at the better hotels continued as a favorite afternoon diversion of the wealthy smart set, however, and classy cabaret dance teams set the style for both dancing and evening wear. By 1914 the turkey trot had become passé. Couples were dancing Irene and Vernon Castle's "Castle Walk," the old maxixe and three variations of the tango. Fleeting favorites were the Aeroplane Waltz, the Negro Drag and Walkin' the Dog. In 1916 bands added guitars and ukuleles to lend aloha atmosphere to a string of Hawaiian-type novelties with titles like "Yacka Hula Hickey Dula" and "Yicki Hacki Wicki Wackie Woo." But the term most Americans were just beginning to be conscious of was a new wicki-wackie word spelled "jass" and "jaz." Some said it came from Chicago. Others said it was an old New Orleans Creole word, meaning "to speed up." A strong case was made for the theory that it first came into use in Vicksburg in 1910 when dancers cheered on Alexander's Ragtime Band with shouts of "Come on, Chazz!"—the "Chazz," or "Chas.," being an abbreviation of Alexander's first name, Charles. Still others maintained that its roots lay in the Arabic *jazib*, "one that allures"; the Hindi *jazba*, meaning "ardent desire"; and *jaiza*, an African tribal term for "the rumble of distant drums."

In spirit, if not in fact, jazz was all these things and more. But speculation as to the origin of its name was cut short by the rumble of distant cannons in Europe. To the accompaniment of stirring song-and-dance hits by Irving Berlin and a versatile hoofer named George M. Cohan, America marched off to war. In servicemen's clubs and cabarets in New York, London, Paris and Pocatello doughboys and gobs grabbed partners and danced to "Goodbye Broadway, Hello France." Early in 1918 the king of the prewar ballroom dancers, Vernon Castle, was killed in a military plane crash. Ragtime and the Castle Walk were "old hat," and the Armistice was celebrated at Reisenweber's New York cabaret to exciting new sounds played by the Original Dixieland Jazz Band. With the new music came new dances. Couples circled the floor with a snappy fox trot, and two girl dancers from Chicago—Gilda Gray and Bee Palmer—introduced the country to a torso-shaking fertility fling called the "Shimmy-Shewabble." Believed to have been "invented" in the bawdy bistros of San Francisco's Barbary Coast, the twentieth-century version of the old breast-knocking saraband gave rise to more cries of indignation than the Kaiser's rape of little Belgium.

In the 1919 edition of the *Ziegfeld Follies*, Bert Williams made a show-stopping plea against Prohibition when he complained that "You Can't Make Your Shimmy Shake on Tea." But in clubs and cabarets the "real stuff" was available to trusted customers, and couples shimmied and fox-trotted on whisky and gin as the band blared "Ain't We Got Fun?" "Oh, boy, I'll say!" was the flapper's giggled rejoinder as she pressed her body tight against her partner for a session of "button shining" on the crowded floor. Corsets were removed in the ladies' room and checked for the rest of the night. "The men won't dance with you if you wear a corset," the girls explained—and neither were the men inclined to dance with a "back number" who refused to "pet" or take a friendly nip of hooch from a fellow's hip flask. "The low-cut gowns, the rolled hose and short skirts are born of the Devil and his angels, and are carrying the present and future generations to chaos and destruction," the president of the University of Florida exclaimed, pointing an accusing finger at the immoral hussies who were to become today's gray-haired grandmothers.

The American phobia against dancers in short skirts was extended to include even the classical ballet tutu of the world-famous Anna Pavlova, whose tours were threatened with banning unless she "chose to wear longer skirts." Defiance of the law and a general conventions-be-damned attitude marked the 1922 appearance of Isadora Duncan, America's barefooted mother of the modern dance, who outraged an audience of Boston blue bloods by dancing in a gauzy red scarf, sans undergarments. "Nudity is truth; it is art," Isadora insisted in a later interview, but the scandal all but wrecked her American career.

Since the demise of the vaudeville Salomes, tap and rhythm dancers had moved into theatrical headline spots and agents classified hoofers according to type: Blackface, White-face, Irish, Dutch, Rough, Neat, Acrobatic or Grotesque. The basic steps of the tap dance had been improvised by southern Negroes from white jigs and clogs, and the names of the jazzed jig steps had a distinctly down-home flavor: Buck, Wing, Flea Hop, Falling off the Log, Hitch Kick, Rubber Legs and the old Soft Shoe. Double soles duplicated the slapstick sound of a poor plantation worker's dance in shoes with loose soles, and the sand dance was born of some long-forgotten shuffle on a gritty cabin floor.

The rhythmic impact of jazz-dancing Negro performers in *Shuffle Along* jogged the Broadway musical stage out of its time-stepping rut, and the Harlem version of a knock-kneed, heel-kicking dance from South Carolina created a new dance craze in the mid-twenties—the Charleston. Strictly for the young and limber, the fast-stepping Charleston came in for its share of condemnation, though perceptive prudes were willing to grant that its breakaway buoyancy had greatly reduced "button shining" and was apt to leave both sheik and sheba more pooped than passionate. Warnings were thundered that the new—and, therefore, immoral—dance would be the downfall of the nation. But even the gloomiest of prophets were taken aback when a group of Charleston-ing Bostonians set up a rhythmic vibration that collapsed the roof of the Pickwick Club, killing fifty.

Less lethal but more "lewd" and "indecent" was the fanny-slapping Black Bottom, a copyrighted creation that was presented as a "new twister" in *George White's Scandals of 1926*. In reply to criticism of its anatomically descriptive title, apologists for the dance explained that the name referred to the muddy bottom of the Suwannee River rather than to dark-skinned rumps. No one accepted the fanciful etymology for a moment, however, and in England the dance was called "The Black Base" —or, with more dubious decorum, "The Black Bed."

Impressed by the commercial possibilities of creating a copyrighted dance craze, showmen and performers conspired to invent a new line of novelty dances, such as the Sugar Foot Strut and the New Low Down. Most were too complicated to catch on, however, and only the Varsity Drag enjoyed a short semester of favor. When young Charles Augustus Lindbergh made his historic solo hop to Paris in 1927, jubilant tin-lizzie pilots and their high-flying flappers fox-trotted to "Lucky Lindy." Prosperity made for positive thinking, and sweet "dansapation" was being pushed by such highly arranged bands as those of Vincent Lopez and the hugely popular "Pops" Whiteman. Three years later, in the wake of the Wall Street Crash, tempos slowed, skirts and hairstyles grew longer, and dancers clung to each other as though for reassurance. For a quick escape from economic anxiety, nothing could beat the supercolossal dance spectacles that Hollywood began dishing up with the advent of sound films in 1929, when Ann Pennington, "the Girl with the Dimpled Knees," was seen to "Tiptoe Through the Tulips" with a bevy of beauteous chorines in *Gold Diggers of Broadway*. Under the direction of Busby Berkley, other girls with dimpled knees, cheeks and chins moved in eye-filling masses to form human fountains. Girls danced out of clouds in wind-blown gauze. Girls kicked and tapped and imitated trains. Whole battalions of girls lay on their backs and were photographed from above as their arms and legs formed floral patterns that changed into wheels and stars.

No less numbing to the senses were the awesome precision drills of the thirty-two girl Rockettes at the Radio City Music Hall. In 1934 New York spectator sports who could afford a first-run movie visited the Music Hall to enjoy the top-hat sophistication of a new Hollywood dance team—Fred Astaire and Ginger Rogers. While the professional intricacies of the Continental and the Carioca were not easily mastered, house-party imitations of the Astaire-Rogers technique were good for laughs, and the musical suggestion of faraway places helped to popularize Latin-American tempos and dances. Though the rumba had already arrived with New York's international set and "The Peanut Vendor" had been a hit in 1931, most Americans approached the seductive Cuban dance as though it were a coochy fox trot.

More to the mass taste was the familiar fox-trot beat of commercial dance bands led by such big-time radio "maestros" as Ben Bernie and Rudy Vallee. Large public ballrooms competed for Depression dollars with big-name bands, while many smaller operators switched to a dime-a-dance policy. Couples were welcome, but the appeal was largely to foot-loose males, who could hire a "glamorous hostess" for a turn around the floor just as they might hire a cab for a spin around the block—for which reason the girls were called "taxi dancers." The dreariest ballroom device, by far, was the dance marathon—an endurance contest in which competing couples danced, walked and stumbled around a dance floor for weeks and months on end. Most marathons were rigged, and all traded on a brand of low-grade show-business hoke that brought audiences back night after night to root for "the brave little kiddies."

Among the major box-office attractions of 1933 was the *Streets of Paris* side show at the Chicago Century of Progress Exposition, where a dancer named Sally Rand was offering glimpses of her pink-toned torso through the artful manipulation of a pair of fluffy plumes. The sensational success of Miss Rand's breezy fan dance touched off an imitative flesh-and-feathers fad among girl performers in the new post-Repeal night clubs, so the resourceful Sally switched to a copyrighted bubble dance for an engagement at Broadway's Paradise Restaurant, where she performed behind a transparent screen to protect her bubbles from the pinpricks of practical jokers at ringside. Less cautious artists continued to shake their fans in the smaller clubs clustered along New York's Fifty-second Street, where they were eventually displaced by groups of fully clothed male musicians who played a new style of jazz called "swing."

Swing, like all earlier jazz, was music for dancing. "Let's Dance" was the theme of the Benny Goodman band, and in the vanguard of the new movement were such robust ballroom veterans as Louis Armstrong, Louis Prima, Fats Waller, Red Norvo, Wingy Manone and Red McKenzie. Slicker and less exciting, perhaps, were the carefully contrived arrangements of Glen Gray, Hal Kemp, Kay Kyser, and the Dorseys. Slick or "hep," the swingy style inspired dancers to cut loose from gliding fox-trot forms, such as the Westchester and Peabody. Couples jumped around the floor in a face-to-face kind of jig called the lindy hop. Crepe-soled saddle shoes gave added bounce and served as shock absorbers for the jazzy jumpers, who soon earned the name of "jitterbugs." Breakaways and fancy swing-outs widened the gap between partners, and the lindy began to resemble a set of related solos danced at arm's length. To the original face-to-face "Shag" motif were added the sideways-shuffling "Suzy-Q" and a tricky little step, with one wagging finger raised, called "Truckin'." Considered new and novel, the strange jitterbug japes elicited the usual expressions of disapproval and despair for modern youth, though every movement the "hepcats" made could be found in the ancient Indian *Natya Sastra*. What was "Peckin'," for instance, but the old *Prakampita*, in which the neck moved backward and forward like a she-pigeon's? "Usage: To denote 'You and I,' folk-dancing, swinging, inarticulate murmurings and the sound uttered by a woman at the time of conjugal embrace."

Jitterbugs were not apt to spend their time browsing through the *Natya Sastra*, however. They swung like "gates," and, as everyone knew, "gate" was a nickname for "alligator." "Greetings, gate!" and "See you later, alligator!" were the hepcat's "hello" and "good-by," and anyone who wasn't "hep to the jive" and preferred sweet music was a sticky "ickey." America was "hoof-nutty," *Variety* reported, citing the fad for a new dance —originated by the Gullah Negroes of the Carolina coast—which required "a lot of floating power and fannying." Called the Big Apple, the short-lived swing dance inspired the creation of the Little Pear and the Little Peach—novelties that proved even more ephemeral than the English "Lambeth Walk."

In 1938 hepcats danced to the humorous sound of "The Flat Foot Floogie"—"with a floy-floy"—but they no longer jived with the same intensity. Couples "cooled their socks" by hanging around the bandstand, listening to musicians improvise, and many went dancing mainly to enjoy the impromptu jam sessions, which Benny Goodman built into a nightly feature with his trio and quartet. While watching Gene Krupa and Lionel Hampton work, dancers were too enthralled to move, and they welcomed the chance to sit down and listen when the Goodman band made its 1938 concert appearance at Carnegie Hall. As the thirties rode to a close, good swing was ear music and no one over fifteen would admit to being a jitterbug. Glenn Miller and Artie Shaw could still put a party in the mood for dancing, but serious students of jazz spent their time listening to old Bix Beiderbecke records.

A 1940 fox trot, called "Six Lessons from Madame La Zonga," extolled the hip-and-knee freedom of the rumba and the conga—the latter an Afro-Cuban chain dance, in which dancers lined up in single file with their hands on the shoulders of the person in front and snaked around the room with a "One, two, three, *kick!*" The conga, while generally popular, was biggest with the café society set, which doted on the Latin exotica of bands like Xavier Cugat's. But when the smart New York clubs shut down for the night, the conga was forgotten. Slumming sophisticates took cabs to Harlem hot spots, where the afterhours' floor show would feature a line of nude chorines.

For devotees of the ancient erotic dance who couldn't afford to stay up all night, the thirties had offered "Continuous Burlesk" with such strip-tease dancing stars as Gypsy Rose Lee, Ann Corio and Margie Hart. Queen of the nonstop grinds was Georgia Sothern, while the breast dance was the muscular specialty of king-sized Carrie Finnell, who could make her bounteous bosoms rotate clockwise and counterclockwise, one at a time or in breath-taking tandem. In New York, big-time "burleycue" was reformed clean out of the theaters in the late thirties, and "exotic" dancers were given World War II asylum in the less successful swing clubs of Fifty-second Street, where they strutted and stripped for the soldier-and-sailor trade.

During the war years, the fox trot, the lindy, the rumba and the waltz served all ranks and serial numbers with an excuse to hold a girl in their arms. Stepwise, all was status quo, save for an occasional outburst of the "Pennsylvania Polka" or "Beer Barrel Polka" and the discovery of the American square dance by eastern G.I.s stationed in the West. The vigorous folk elements of the square dance were corralled by Agnes de Mille in her cowboy ballet, *Rodeo*—a rousing 1942 success that earned her the choreographic assignment for the Broadway musical, *Oklahoma!* Similarly, the big-city jazz style of Jerome Robbins' ballet, *Fancy Free,* was apparent in his choreography for the 1944 musical hit, *On the Town.* Equally urban and unique was the characterization Gene Kelly tapped out in the title role of *Pal Joey,* and wartime moviegoers applauded his Hollywood dancing debut with Judy Garland. Teamed with Fred Astaire, the glamorous Rita Hayworth drew wolf whistles from armed-forces audiences, as did the lithesome legwork of blond Betty Grable, whose photo in G.I. footlockers qualified her for the role of America's favorite pin-up girl.

Victory in Europe and Japan did nothing to diminish the American interest in pretty dancing girls, but the postwar period was far from hoof-nutty. Among avant-garde musicians, the wartime beat of boogiewoogie was replaced by the improvised non sequiturs of bebop—an introspective kind of jumpless jazz that left dancers flat-footed. The new hepcats, now called "hipsters," didn't dance. They "dug the sounds" and "cooled it" with an occasional shrug or finger snap. The physical and emotional responses that dancing required were neo-ickey, or "square"—as were the "nowhere" audiences who were picking up on the classical ballet kick and the aging jitterbugs of yesteryear who sat at home with their new TV sets, bemused by the choreography of cigarettes and beer cans in the animated commercials.

Ballrooms, bands and night clubs went into a state of

economic collapse. In New York, a growing Puerto Rican population supported a small number of ballrooms specializing in the Brazilian samba, the Cuban mambo and the Dominican merengue—dances which North American dance instructors adapted for mass consumption. But most of the country had laughed off Latin tempos with "South America, Take It Away," and mainland club owners of the early fifties couldn't even count on the cultish devotion of the few to keep a small rumba band working. The new no-dance jazz thrived modestly on recordings issued by small record companies, while big record companies cut their dance-disc output to a minimum and plugged for million-copy sales with recordings by name vocalists. By 1953, the disastrous unemployment situation among dance-band musicians led *Down Beat* magazine to launch a campaign to promote dancing on the college and high-school levels. "Kids Don't Know How to Dance," a headline quoted bandleader Stan Kenton as saying. "Every place we played during the past year, I noticed that the younger couples, for the most part, didn't seem to know what they were doing on the floor—particularly when we played numbers with any real beat, rhythm things that really jumped." In ensuing weeks and months, all sorts of remedies were suggested, but the ultimate cure lay in the bottom category of *Down Beat's* biweekly breakdown of new record releases: "Rhythm and Blues."

In 1953 the rhythm-and-blues classification served to segregate the solid, rolling beat of Negro popular music from the integrated upper echelons of "jazz" and the white-angled arrangements of the commercially "popular." Its performers were mostly unknown, and titles like "Brown-Skin Butterball," "Poon Tang" and "Rock, Rock, Rock" were played by small-station disc jockeys who aimed at the Negro market. When it became apparent that teen-agers of all races were tuning in on the rowdy record shows, white "dee-jays" began spinning the same forty-fives. The rhythms were so compelling that dancers couldn't help rocking, and when the racial distinctions of rhythm-and-blues broke down, the rolling two-beat tempo and all its lindy-based dance variations were lumped together as "rock 'n' roll."

Parents, teachers, religious leaders and trained musicians protested the new "barbarism," but, from a historical point of view, rock 'n' roll represented a healthy revitalization of the age-old urge to dance. By late 1956, record companies were working on three shifts to satisfy the multimillion-dollar demand for rock-'n'-roll records, dancing schools reported an upsurge in business, and rug manufacturers noted a trend to area rugs that could be rolled up for dancing. A quickie, low-budget film called *Rock Around the Clock* rang up a $3,000,000 profit; and when the New York Paramount Theatre combined the premiere of *Don't Knock the Rock* with a rock-'n'-roll stage show, teen-age fans began lining up at the box office at four A.M. The riotous behavior of fans in Boston and other cities made rock 'n' roll synonymous with juvenile delinquency, but the new American tempo struck a responsive chord with rhythm-hungry young people the world over. Within a year, England, France, Germany and Japan began to develop their own rock-'n'-roll music and Russian youths were beating it out high, wide and Amerikanski to black-market recordings of "Hound Dog" cut on old X-ray plates.

In 1959 Soviet authorities were still denouncing the Russian rock-'n'-rollers as "lizards," "toadstools" and dupes of the American Central Intelligence Agency when the then Premier Khrushchev startled the Western world with a front-page rebuke to Hollywood for inviting him to witness the filming of a modestly dressed version of the can-can. According to dancing star Shirley MacLaine, however, Khrushchev really enjoyed watching the old French dance but hadn't dared to admit it because Mrs. K. was present and frowning. "He may bang his U.N. desk with his shoe," Miss MacLaine mused, "but, just like any other husband, he chickens out when his wife catches him getting too bright-eyed—girlwise."

In shopping around for old dances to censure, the Khrushchevs, or any other visitors to America, could have taken their pick of just about every sex-inspired dance the world has ever produced. With a little briefing on symbolic gestures, Americans and their guests could sit in a state of perpetual shock at ethnic dance recitals featuring obscure fertility motifs from Europe, India, Africa, Polynesia and the East and West Indies. Night clubs and hotel rooms offered opportunities to become outraged over the Hawaiian hula. The ancient North African belly dance invited outbursts of indignation several times nightly in the restaurants of Manhattan's "Greek town." A visit to any ballroom was almost certain to be rewarded with suggestive demonstrations of the latest Latin-American variations on the old Hispano-Indian saraband, the pachanga and the cha-cha—the first a courtship caper in which the gentleman gallops off on a make-believe pony and the second a funsy offshoot of the fertility-charged mambo. On the stage and in motion pictures, ballerinas in brief tutus performed dance dramas that had their origins in the kissing, teasing boy-girl *balleti* of the fifteenth century. And, if this weren't enough, there was still the whole barefooted, Freudian field of the modern art dance that had sprung up since Isadora Duncan's early experiments with neo-Grecian scarves.

The fact that all such dance forms were no longer shocking to Americans may be attributed to the speed with which dances tend to become assimilated into the culture. Persons who were pained by the primitivism of rock 'n' roll one year were anxiously phoning ticket brokers twelve months later, in the hope of procuring a couple of seats to Broadway's "rock-'n'-roll" version of the Romeo-and-Juliet romance, *West Side Story*. A couple of years later, in October, 1961, many of the same cultured crowd could be found standing in line outside a noisy little rock-'n'-roll rendezvous on New York's West Forty-fifth Street, impatiently waiting for a chance to get inside and dance a new shimmy-shewabbling hootchy-kootchy called the "twist."

With the twist, the history of dancing breaks into the bold, black print of recent headlines: Gay Night Club Dervishes Twist. . . . Café Society Voyages West of Fifth Avenue to Pursue Fad—Peppermint Lounge Provides Required Rock 'n' Roll. . . . Governor Twists to Keep Fit. . . . New Jersey Teen-Ager Twists 18 Hours. . . . Sophia's Twist Gave Studio Gang a Turn. . . . The

Twist Takes Washington. . . . Jackie Twists. . . . Meg Gives Twist Royal Treatment at Palace Ball. . . . In Paris It's "le Tweest". . . . Warsaw Wiggles. . . . Twisters Give Tokyo New Tremors." As the flash bulbs popped and reporters scurried to scoop the names of notables seen twisting at the Peppermint Lounge, the history of the twist was already being snowed under by a blizzard of publicity releases. Among the more-or-less verifiable data was the fact that a rock-'n'-roll singer named Hank Ballard had recorded a song called "The Twist" five years before and that a young singer from Philadelphia, who worked under the *nom de disc* of Chubby Checker, had been plugging the song and dance around the country. Amidst all the fanny-shaking rumpus, other old-time Philadelphians of eighteen and nineteen recalled doing the twist in their youth, when it was a purely local phenomenon known as the Madison.

The facts, shaky as they were, ended there. But in the fall of 1961 the twist was making history by the minute. Never since the beginning of time had a dance craze spread so rapidly and through so many levels of society. At the Peppermint Lounge and the Wagon Wheel, kids in jeans and toreador pants were given the hip by VIP posteriors and socially prominent derrieres. Class distinctions and cultural barriers were twisted down overnight, and a group of leading psychiatrists assured *The New York Times* that the elbow-rubbing between masses and classes bottomed out with a great big plus, mental-health-wise. "It's a good way to work off tension," explained a twisting Wall Street broker with a daytime seat on the Stock Exchange. "If I couldn't do the Twist, I'd die," a waitress confided while serving up a Mashed-Potato wiggle.

Within a very few weeks, the twist was indistinguishable from the ultrasocial whirl. At the charitable April in Paris Ball (held in October in New York), dancers dined and twisted at a nifty $150 a head. In the first week of November, another white-tie twist party was thrown for the benefit of homeless girls, and two weeks later "silk-clad bodies and diamonds shimmered to the music of the Twist" at a benefit bash held at the Metropolitan Museum of Art. In granting permission for the fete, the museum's director, James J. Rorimer, had evidently anticipated the usual fox trots, waltzes and rumbas. When he arrived to find the trimly girdled assemblage twisting round and round to the blaring sounds of "Fanny May" and "You Can't Sit Down," he reportedly "shook with dismay and horror." And when "he saw the photographers hastening to photograph the guests doing the Twist in the shrine of Rembrandt and Cezanne," Mr. Rorimer objected. "I did not invite them," he shouted. "I was not aware of this!" But if the Rembrandts, Cezannes, Brueghels and Egyptian mummies could have stepped down out of their frames and cases, it most certainly would have been not to rout the revelers from the museum's hallowed halls but to join in the fun—for there was nothing about the twist that the old Flemish peasants and ancient Egyptians had not known in their own *Hoppeldeis* and *hbjs*.

As it was in the Old Kingdom of the Nile, so it was in the capital of the New Frontier on the Potomac. Top-level twist parties were tossed by European ministers, ambassadors from the Near East and members of the President's Cabinet. The twist was diplomatically danced by officials of the State Department, visiting dignitaries, Congressional whips and big-brass strategists from the Pentagon. When, on a festive evening in February, 1962, the First Lady twisted with the Secretary of Defense beneath the historic old crystal chandeliers of the White House Blue Room, the dance became as much a part of our national heritage as "Hail, Columbia" and Paul Revere's ride.

While the late President Kennedy was never known to do the twist, the family's favorite bandleader, Lester Lanin, has been quoted as saying that he liked "good, spirited cheerful dance music." The President didn't dance often, Mr. Lanin said, and when he did it was only for a few minutes at a time—possibly as a result of his painful back injury.

During his tragically brief period in office, John F. Kennedy made no public statement on dancing, but his predecessor, Dwight D. Eisenhower, chose the occasion of the Eisenhower Library dedication in Abilene, Kansas, to make his own views known. "We venerate the pioneers who fought droughts and floods, isolation and Indians, to come to Kansas and westward to settle into their homes, to till the soil and raise their families," Mr. Eisenhower stated, by way of preface. "We think of their sturdiness, their self-reliance, their faith in God, we think of their glorious pride in America. Now, I wonder if some of those people could come back today and see us doing the twist instead of the minuet—whether they would be particularly struck by the beauty of that dance?"

Coming when it did, in the twist-mad spring of 1962, the Eisenhower statement gave many thoughtful Americans pause. Certainly the opinion of any group of people who had fought so hard and endured so much in order to live in Kansas would be worthy of our deepest respect —even awe. But unless the history of American dancing is in error, it would seem extremely doubtful that many of the muddy-booted forty-niners who first settled the Cornflower State had ever seen a minuet, much less danced one. While lively reels and jigs were esteemed for their gaiety, the dainty steps of eighteenth-century Versailles would have been as out of place at a frontier dance as French perfume in a crock of corn likker. The vigorous, no-nonsense twist, on the other hand, could have been adapted to life on the western prairies as easily as it was adapted to life in Samoa and Japan. Besides hoeing down such familiar forms as the Fly, the Mashed Potato and the Slop, our fun-loving forefathers might have come up with an "Arkansaw Twist," "Ladies' Choice—Twist or Swing," "Twist Quadrille"—or, perhaps, a variation that we loose-living moderns would never have even thought of: the "Kiss Twist."

No possibility, past or present, seems too farfetched in the light of a report that German twisters had made a hit of a classically based "Liebestraum von Liszt Twist" and that African and West Indian students were teaching the customers of West Berlin's Eden Saloon "a ritualistic 'voodoo twist.' " The Latin-American influence was evident in the pachanga twist and the cha-cha twist, and a

Spanish dance troupe worked out a flamenco twist, which put the heel-toe-rapping routine back in the old Canary Islands fertility groove where the Spanish conquistadors had originally found it in the sixteenth century. For historical perspective, few observations were more to the point than those of the rebellious young Russian poet, Yevgeny Yevtushenko. "The twist is advertised as a miracle of the atomic era," he said in a Moscow interview. "But I remembered Ghana jungles two years ago where I watched African tribal dances. Those dances have existed thousands of years. They were ritual dances that had not yet been called the twist. This miracle of the atomic era is merely a modernized version of what was invented thousands of years ago."

Yevtushenko's comments were made in the face of official Soviet attacks upon the twist and rock 'n' roll as "typical products of capitalist society." "I do not understand how dances can be divided into capitalist and socialist," the poet argued, and suggested that it was perfectly possible for the proletariat to perform the twist "in a pleasing manner." Whether his reasoning had any direct effect on Soviet thinking, it's impossible to say. Four days later, however, Khrushchev put in an appearance at Moscow's Central Sports Arena to hear the touring Benny Goodman band play a concert of American swing. "I enjoyed it," he remarked with surprising mildness. "I don't dance myself, so I don't understand these things too well."

In view of Khrushchev's apparent tolerance toward Western dance music of the thirties, admirers of the Russian dance found some small reason to hope that

Moscow would one day be as receptive toward new dances as it has been zealous in preserving the traditional Russian folk and ballet forms. But if the past be any guide, conservatives of all nations will continue to greet the new and novel with cries of outrage and alarm. What will the next shocker be like? We wonder. Can we look for a revival of "smouching" and under-the-girdle lady-lifting? Or will American social dancing go cool and neoclassical with button-down *balleti* and organization-man minuets?

In the fall of 1964 there were no clear indications of what the future might bring. The bossa nova, a jazz switch on the old Brazilian samba, had created a brief flurry of excitement during the previous year. President Lyndon B. Johnson, easily the most tireless and determined dancer ever to occupy the White House, was described by his numerous partners as "a good waltz man." The original twist had become as prosaic as the polka, but malt-shop maidens and jukebox bucks continued to wiggle and shake out new variations with a strong jungle beat—the Hully Gully, the Wobble, the Surf, the Popeye, the Frankenstein, the Barrel, the Bug, the Frug, the Shake and the Watusi. African diplomats from the newly independent nations had introduced the attaché-case cadre to the genteel understatements of the High Life—a slow and easy souvenir from colonial days on the Gold Coast—and G. Mennen Williams, Assistant Secretary for African Affairs, invited 160 envoys from Africa to a square-dance hoedown at the State Department in Washington, where the colloquial calls of the "Quadrille Américain" had to be translated into diplomatic French in order to be understood by the Secretary's guests—thus bringing the circle full round to the early 1800's, when "sashay" was spelled *chassé* and *dos-à-dos* became "do-si-do."

In Paris, London, New York and Los Angeles, meanwhile, members of the jet set were Frugging and Bugging on the crowded, dime-size dance floors of their new and exclusive *discothèques*—vodka-Martini versions of the teen-age malt shop, where live disc jockeys supplanted jukeboxes and couples danced out storytelling charades, such as the Bird, the Pony, the Snake, the Monkey, the Hitchhiker and the Heat Wave. "Like the Twist, most *discothèque* dancing keeps partners apart," *Time* magazine reported, "but on the West Coast they are discovering that there is something to be said for ventroventral variations. Such are the Dog, the Fish and the Swim, which has been banned in at least one California high school. And such is the newest—the GoGo."

In the GoGo, the head "arcs back and forth, the arms chop up and down, the feet are planted. And the bodies, glued together abdomen to abdomen, endlessly twist, twitch and bounce" in a button-shining fertility routine whose basic purpose might be more readily served if the dancers came clad in a thin layer of body paint.

Which brings us back to our original question: What will the future bring? Will the GoGo be refined into some playfully innocent "Eskimo Pie" in which dancers wearing bulky coats will hold hands and rub noses? Or will it lead to increasingly erotic forms—the Going-Going and the GoneGone?

In his imaginative projection of the *Brave New World*

of the future, Aldous Huxley once described the dance of tomorrow as a kind of carnal conga performed in the buff—the "Orgy-porgy." "Round they went, a circular procession of dancers, each with hands on the hips of the dancer preceding, round and round, shouting in unison, stamping to the rhythm of the music with their feet; beating it, beating it out with hands on the buttocks in front; twelve pairs of hands beating as one; as one, twelve buttocks slabbily resounding . . .

> "*Orgy-porgy, Ford and fun,*
> *Kiss the girls and make them One.*
> *Boys at one with girls at peace;*
> *Orgy-porgy gives release.*"

Huxley could have been wrong, of course, but the history of dancing indicates that his prophecy may yet come true—in which case no one who has done his homework on the subject should be the least bit surprised. But if we—the sturdy, self-reliant pioneers of the early Space Age—were to come back and find our descendants doing the Orgy-porgy instead of the GoGo, the Watusi and the Frug—would we be particularly struck with the beauty of that dance? Would we join our Puritan ancestors in setting up a ghostly howl against "ye madd Bacchanalians"? Or would we accept the Orgy-porgy in the spirit of the Cobéua Indians of Brazil and help "carry the fertility into every corner of the houses, to the edge of the woods, to the nearby fields" with cheerful grunts of "*ai (ye)—ai (ye)—ai (ye)!*"

INDEX